ENGLAND
UNLOCKED

by

Tessa Girvan

illustrations by

Katherine Hardy & Victoria Scott

edited by

Emily Kerr & Joshua Perry

This book belongs to:

CONTENTS

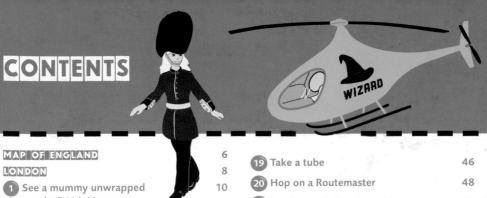

LONDON

SOUTH EAST

SOUTH WEST

EAST

MIDLANDS

NORTH EAST

NORTH WEST

TOP FIVES

CONTENTS

I ♥ whitby

HADRIAN WOZ 'ERE CXXI

LONDON

SOUTH EAST

SOUTH WEST

EAST

MIDLANDS

NORTH EAST

NORTH WEST

TOP FIVES

LONDON
SOUTH EAST
SOUTH WEST
EAST
MIDLANDS
NORTH EAST
NORTH WEST
TOP FIVES

LONDON

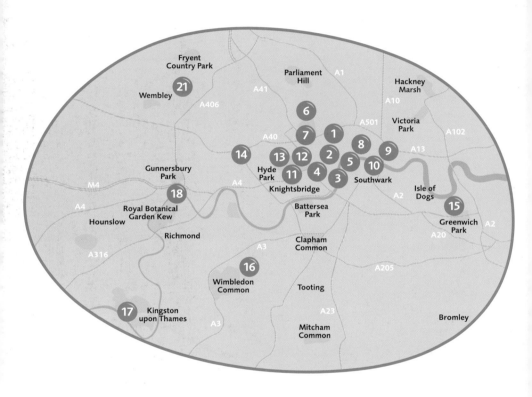

Fryent
Country Park

Wembley **21**

Parliament
Hill

A1

Hackney
Marsh

A41

A406

A10

Victoria
Park

A102

A501

6

7 **1**

A40

8

9

A13

14 **13** **12** **2** **5** **10**

Hyde
Park

11 **4** **3**

Knightsbridge

Southwark

Gunnersbury
Park

A2

Isle of
Dogs

M4

18

A4

Royal Botanical
Garden Kew

Battersea
Park

Greenwich
Park

15

A2

Hounslow

A4

Richmond

Clapham
Common

A20

A316

A3

A205

16

Wimbledon
Common

Tooting

17

Kingston
upon Thames

A23

Bromley

A3

Mitcham
Common

KEY

 Places

 Parks

 River

SOUTH EAST

SOUTH WEST

EAST

MIDLANDS

NORTH EAST

NORTH WEST

TOP FIVES

SEE A MUMMY UNWRAPPED

...at the British Museum

Like everyone, the British Museum loves its mummy. However, in this case we're talking about *3,000 year old Egyptian mummies.*

Mummies were made by removing a dead person's insides, wrapping the corpse in linen and gooey resin, then putting it in a fancy coffin. Opening a mummy's coffin can cause damage, so it's rare to catch a glimpse of one. But the museum has got round this by exhibiting several mummies in different states of unwrap. There are also some mummified cats, and even a falcon.

Sticker Scores

5 PERFECT PYRAMID

4 TERRIFIC TOMB

3 COMMON CASKET

2 CURSED COFFIN

1 I WANT MY MUMMY

Best of the Rest

🔑 See the famous Rosetta Stone. The stone is engraved with text carved in several ancient languages, and its discovery in 1799 helped researchers understand hieroglyphics (Egyptian writing).

🔑 Discover the 2,500 year old Elgin Marbles. The marbles are sculptures of Greek gods and other mythological figures, and there's controversy over whether they should be in the museum. The Greeks think they were taken illegally and want them returned to Athens.

Make A Day Of It

🔑 Hop over to France on the super-speedy Eurostar train. It leaves from nearby St Pancras station and goes through the Channel Tunnel. Within two and a half hours you'll be in the centre of Paris! www.eurostar.com

Fascinating Facts

★ **The name mummy comes from the Arabic word mummia, which means tar. The Arabs who first saw the tombs called the bodies this because they were covered in black sticky stuff.**

★ Egyptian embalmers used special tools to remove a body's internal organs. To get the brain out they would stick a hook in through the corpse's nostrils, as if they were picking its nose. It is not known if they then ate the bogeys!

How do you make a mummy dance?

Play it some *wrap* music!

PLAN YOUR VISIT ①

British Museum
Great Russell Street, WC1B 3DG
www.britishmuseum.org

📞 020 7323 8000
🕐 Daily 10.30-17.30
⊖ Holborn / Tottenham Court Road

FREE

I want to go here ☐

↙ The British Museum's Great Court

FIND THE WORLD'S SMALLEST POLIC

...in Trafalgar Square

Barely big enough for one policeman, the world's smallest police station is located inside a lamppost on Trafalgar Square in Central London.

It was originally built as a lookout post so police (or one of them at least) could keep a close eye on any riots and demonstrations that took place in the square. It contained a direct telephone line to the police headquarters at Scotland Yard, so reinforcements could be swiftly summoned when needed. Nowadays the tiny police station is used as a storage cupboard by cleaners!

How do pigeons tell the time?

With a *coo-coo* clock!

POLICE STATION

Sticker Scores

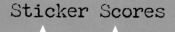

5	4	3
STAR SUPERINTENDENT	IMPORTANT INSPECTOR	SENIOR SERGEANT

2	1
COMPETENT CONSTABLE	BUNGLING BURGLAR

Photo Op
Lounge like a lion beside Nelson's Column! Look at the lions at the bottom of the column and copy their pose. *Roaarrr!*

TATION

Make A Day Of It

🔑 Catch a musical in the West End. Head to the TKTS booth on Leicester Square on the day you want to see a show – you can often get half-price tickets. Be careful you go to the right place – TKTS is the only official ticket booth on the square. www.londontheatre.co.uk

🔑 Ice skate in an eighteenth-century courtyard. Between November and January each year, Somerset House is the site of a *cool* outdoor ice rink. Beginners' lessons are available, so you'll be gliding along n-*ice*-ly in no time! www.somersethouse.org.uk

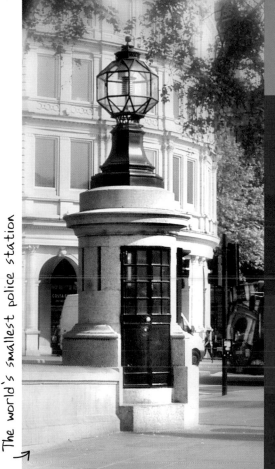

The world's smallest police station

Fascinating Facts

⭐ Trafalgar Square has its very own police hawk! The square's resident pigeons can cause damage and pester tourists, so the hawk is under orders to scare away troublesome customers.

⭐ On the inside of Admiralty Arch (south-west of Trafalgar Square) you'll find a carved nose, one metre above adult head height. It was stuck on by an artist called Rick Buckley in 1997. Goodness *nose* why he did it!

PLAN YOUR VISIT ②

Trafalgar Square
Trafalgar Square, WC2
www.london.gov.uk/trafalgarsquare
⊖ Charing Cross
FREE

I want to go here ☐

HEAR BIG BEN'S BONGS

...at Westminster Palace

Big Ben is the name people give to the giant clock tower attached to the Houses of Parliament. However, originally Big Ben was really the nickname of the big, bongtastic bell inside the tower.

The building is officially called St Stephen's Tower and is one of the most famous sights in London. Despite being over 150 years old, the clock is incredibly reliable. The main bell rings every hour on the hour, and four smaller bells chime every fifteen minutes. For the best bonging experience listen at midday so you can hear twelve bongs in a row.

Sticker Scores

5	4	3
ATOMIC CLOCK	QUARTZ WATCH	STOPWATCH

2	1
SUNDIAL	EGG TIMER

Fascinating Facts

★ In 1949 Big Ben was delayed by four and a half minutes when a big flock of starlings perched on the minute hand of the clock. The weight of the birds stopped the hand from turning. Unfortunately, blaming the starlings is unlikely to work when you're late for a maths lesson!

★ The secret to the clock's top timekeeping lies in a stack of old penny coins that sits on top of its pendulum. The pennies adjust the weight of the pendulum, affecting the speed at which it swings. Adding or removing one penny alters the time by 0.4 seconds a day.

★ The bell weighs around fourteen tonnes. That means it's as heavy as 165,000 starlings (but much less likely to fly away).

Make A Day Of It

🔑 Create your own art at the Tate Britain. There are roving art trolleys with materials for making your own masterpiece. www.tate.org.uk

Bongtastic Big Ben

PLAN YOUR VISIT ③

Big Ben
The Palace of Westminster, Westminster, SW1A 0AA

www.parliament.uk/bigben

⊖ Westminster

FREE

I want to go here ☐

Photo Op
If you get the angles right you can take a photo which makes it look like you're leaning against Big Ben. Stand with the tower in the background and hold your hand out so that from the camera's viewpoint it looks like Big Ben is supporting your weight.

MARCH WITH SOLDIERS

...outside Buckingham Palace

Lots of important people have bodyguards. But the Queen is the only person in the country to have her very own selection of soldiers.

The Queen's Guard is made up of soldiers with big guns and furry hats. Their job is to protect the Queen when she's at home. They take it in turns to guard her, and the ceremony where they swap over is called the Changing of the Guard.

There are several good places to watch the Changing of the Guard. Start at Horse Guards Arch at 11.00, where you can see the cavalry (soldiers on horseback) change over. Then dash to Wellington Barracks on Birdcage Walk and watch the band play as the new guard gets ready. Finally, march alongside the changing soldiers as they head towards Buckingham Palace.

Sticker Scores

☆ 5	☆ 4	☆ 3
QUEEN'S GUARD	BODYGUARD	SECURITY GUARD

☆ 2	☆ 1
LIFE GUARD	MOUTH GUARD

Best of the Rest

🔑 Visit The Guards Museum on nearby Birdcage Walk (a great option if it's raining outside!). You can try on a bearskin hat, and it's free to get in if you're under sixteen.

🔑 Bring some bird-seed and feed the ducks in the lake in St James's Park, which is next to the palace.

Top Tip
The Changing of the Guard doesn't take place every day (and it can be postponed if it's raining), so check online for timings before you visit.

Fascinating Facts

⭐ There are five different infantry regiments in the Queen's Guard: Grenadier Guards, Coldstream Guards, Scots Guards, Irish Guards and Welsh Guards. Each regiment has its own uniform.

⭐ Henry VIII designed St James's Park as a private playground for the royal family. When James I came to the throne he stocked it with exotic animals, including camels, crocodiles and even an elephant! So the public were probably happy that it was surrounded by a high brick wall!

Photo Op
Have your picture taken next to a member of the Queen's Guard. There's one standing on his own near St James's Palace.

Aargh, I can't see where I'm going!

PLAN YOUR VISIT ④

Changing of the Guard

Buckingham Palace, Horse Guards Arch and Wellington Barracks, SW1

www.changing-the-guard.com (unofficial website)

🕐 Selected days 11.00

⊖ Charing Cross for Horse Guards Arch, Victoria for Buckingham Palace

FREE

I want to go here ☐

PLAY I-SPY IN THE SKY

...on the London Eye

Everyone loves a game of I-spy, but it's best when there's lots to see. So there's no better place to play than the **London Eye**, where you can check out some of London's finest views.

The London Eye is also known as the Millennium Wheel, because it opened to the public on the last day of 1999 to celebrate the new millennium. It's a gigantic observation wheel, which lifts you off the ground and takes you around a giant loop in the sky.

The views from the Eye are spectacular – on a clear day you can see as far as Windsor Castle, which is 25 miles away! You could try spying Big Ben, St Paul's Cathedral or Buckingham Palace as they're all visible during your journey.

Sticker Scores

5 BIG WHEEL

4 ENTICING EYE

3 FAIR FERRIS

2 RUBBISH RIDE

1 *WHEELY DISAPPOINTING*

Make A Day Of It

 Gawp at the biggest cinema screen in the UK, at the BFI IMAX. It covers the same amount of space as 1,000 widescreen televisions! You watch the films through a special pair of glasses, to get a thrilling 3-D effect. www.bfi.org.uk

 See sharks swim beneath your feet on the floating glass platform at the Sea Life London Aquarium. www.sealife.co.uk/london

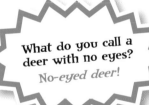

What do you call a deer with no eyes?
No-*eyed deer!*

I spy with my little eye something beginning with . . . .

Fascinating Facts

⭐ There are 32 glass passenger capsules on the London Eye. Each capsule weighs ten tonnes, which is the same as over one million pound coins (but less likely to make you a millionaire!).

⭐ The London Eye measures 135 metres from top to bottom, which is taller (but less gruesome) than a stack of 5,500 real eyes.

PLAN YOUR VISIT ⑤

The Merlin Entertainments London Eye

County Hall, Westminster Bridge Road, SE1 7PB
www.londoneye.com

📞 0871 781 3000

🕐 Daily (summer) 10.00-21.00
Daily (out of season) 10.00-20.30
Opening hours can vary during school holidays

⊖ Westminster / Waterloo

£££ ❌ 🎁

I want to go here ☐

WATCH PENGUINS BEING FED

...at ZSL London Zoo

London Zoo is home to over 750 different species. And, as animals can't cook, they all need feeding. You can watch many of the animals being fed, but the peckish penguins are particularly popular.

ZSL London Zoo is located in the city's Regents Park. It's the world's oldest scientific zoo, which means that it was originally used by scientists to study species. You'll see all kinds of animals including gentle giraffes, giant Galapagos tortoises and mysterious moon jellyfish. Londoners are lucky that they still have a zoo – it nearly closed down in 1991 but thankfully public support kept it open.

Try and watch the patient penguins at dinner time. They line up in an orderly queue, waiting to be fed. It's a s-*peck*-tacular sight!

Sticker Scores

5 PERFECT PENGUINS

4 GREAT GORILLAS

3 BRILLIANT BIRDS

2 REASONABLE REPTILES

1 PUNY PLANKTON

Best of the Rest

 Explore underground tunnels in the Animal Adventure part of the zoo. You can also splash in the water zone and traipse through tree tops.

 Admire butterflies from around the world in the caterpillar-shaped Butterfly Paradise.

Make A Day Of It

 Hire a pedalo in Regent's Park. There's a lake for children only, but you can hire a bigger pedalo or rowing boat if you're with an energetic adult. www.royalparks.gov.uk/The-Regents-Park

↳ single file, please!

What do penguins eat for lunch?
Ice berg-ers!

Fascinating Facts

★ **Penguins eat up to one kilogram of fish each day, and they swallow each fish in a single gulp (we do the same with chocolate cake!).**

★ Many animals have funny names to describe a group of them. For example, you would say a pride of lions, a tower of giraffes, or a crash of rhinoceroses. A collection of penguins is usually called a colony.

★ **When a flea jumps, it accelerates twenty times faster than a space rocket. Sadly, scientists have not yet found a way to take advantage of this – if you strap a shuttle onto a flea's back you're unlikely to end up on the moon.**

PLAN YOUR VISIT 6

ZSL London Zoo
Outer Circle, Regent's Park, NW1 4RY
www.zsl.org

 0844 225 1826

🕐 **Daily (summer) 10.00-17.30
Closes earlier out of season**

⊖ **Camden Town / St. John's Wood**

£££

I want to go here ☐

MEET BECKS AND BEYONCÉ

...at Madame Tussauds

Have you ever wanted to meet your heroes? Well, at Madame Tussauds you can. Just so long as you don't mind them being made of wax!

Madame Marie Tussaud was a wax modeller from France. She opened her museum containing creepily accurate wax copies of famous people in London in 1835. Back then she focused on well-known leaders and explorers, whereas nowadays you'll find everyone from sports stars to royals to rock idols.

David Beckham and Beyoncé are two of the most popular exhibits, but if they don't excite you there are hundreds of others to choose from. OK, so they might not be the *real* stars, but they do make for great photos!

Sticker Scores

5 HOLLYWOOD HERO

4 ROCK LEGEND

3 SOAP STAR

2 X FACTOR CONTESTANT

1 BIG BROTHER WANNABE

Best of the Rest

Take a terrific track through London's history on the Spirit of London ride. You'll see Shakespeare write, watch the Great Fire of 1666 and experience the swinging 60s.

Have your photo taken with the Queen on the Royal Balcony.

Top Tip
The attraction is very popular and there's often a long wait to get in, so get there early if you can!

← Which one s the wax figure?

Fascinating Facts

★ **During the French Revolution, Madame Tussaud searched through the corpses of people whose heads had been chopped off and made wax masks from her favourites. This is not a hobby we would recommend.**

★ Each wax figure takes about four months to make and costs around £150,000. That's enough to buy 300,000 Mars bars (or one mid-range Ferrari).

Photo Op
You won't need any help taking fun photos at Madame Tussauds – every wax figure is a potential super-snap!

PLAN YOUR VISIT 7

Madame Tussauds
Marylebone Road, NW1 5LR
www.madametussauds.com

☏ 0871 894 3000

🕐 **Daily 09.30-17.30 (opens extended hours at peak times)**

⊖ Baker Street

£££

I want to go here ☐

The image depicts a wax figure owned and created by Madame Tussauds

23

WALK AROUND A WHISPERING GALLERY

...at St Paul's Cathedral

Have you ever wanted to be able to hear a whisper on the other side of a room just like some of your teachers? Well, now you can, by visiting the whispering gallery at St Paul's Cathedral.

The cathedral was built after the Great Fire of London in 1666. It's best known for its big dome, which was inspired by the Catholic Church of St Peter in Rome. This was controversial, since being Catholic in England was generally discouraged at this time and often led to you being burned to death! Inside the dome, you can climb up a spiral staircase to reach the whispering gallery. Its perfectly round shape means you can hear someone whispering over on the other side of the room. So be careful what you say!

Why are tombs always unwell?
Because they keep *coffin!*

Sticker Scores

5 DELIGHTFUL DOME

4 SPECTACULAR SPHERE

3 REMARKABLE ROOF

2 CURVY CEILING

1 LEAKY TENT

Inside the dome of St Paul's Cathedral

Best of the Rest

🔑 Get a 360 degree view across London from the Golden Gallery at the top of the dome.

🔑 Search for the tombs of famous people. Good ones to look out for include the graves of Horatio Nelson, Florence Nightingale and the architect of St Paul's Cathedral, Sir Christopher Wren.

Make A Day Of It

🔑 Climb 311 steps to the top of the Monument. It was built to commemorate the Great Fire of London, and was also designed by Sir Christopher Wren.
www.themonument.info

Fascinating Facts

⭐ **The Great Fire of London started in a bakery in the appropriately named Pudding Lane, right in the centre of London. The fire destroyed most of the city, which then had to be almost totally rebuilt.**

⭐ The dome measures 108 metres from top to bottom. That's taller than 140 penguins standing on top of each other (but less likely to topple over!).

⭐ **For years, only towns that had a cathedral in them were granted the status of city. To get an upgrade these days, towns simply need to have a few hundred thousand residents and ask the Queen nicely.**

PLAN YOUR VISIT ⑧

St Paul's Cathedral
St Paul's Churchyard, EC4M 8AD
www.stpauls.co.uk

📞 **020 7236 4128**

🕐 **Mon-Sat 08.30-16.00**
Closed for special services

🚇 St Paul's

I want to go here ☐

CHECK OUT THE CROWN JEWELS

...at the Tower of London

Most people store their jewellery in a box. The royal family go several steps further. They keep theirs in a box, in a house, in a tower, surrounded by a moat and guarded by soldiers *and* birds!

The Crown Jewels are kept safely under lock and key (and behind thick glass) in the Tower of London's Jewel House. They've been there for over 700 years, and are only taken out when they're needed by kings and queens for special royal events. As well as a selection of crowns, you'll also see orbs (round balls) sceptres (long sticks) and swords. But be warned; only royals can get away with a sword as an accessory for their party outfit!

Sticker Scores

5 — DIAMOND CROWN

4 — JEWELLED SCEPTRE

3 — GOLDEN SWORD

2 — ORDINARY ORB

1 — PLASTIC BRACELET

Best of the Rest

🔑 Tower above the Thames on Tower Bridge. This magnificent double-decker structure is one of the most recognisable landmarks in London. The upper level is a pedestrian crossing with amazing views, while the lower level is a busy road bridge. Famously, it also splits in two: both sides of the road bridge swing upwards until they are almost vertical, so that boats can glide through. Check the website for a schedule of planned bridge lift times. www.towerbridge.org.uk

Photo Op
Snap yourself posing with a Beefeater in full costume.

Beefeaters guarding the Crown Jewels

Fascinating Facts

⭐ **Officially, the guardians of the Tower are called the Yeoman Warders, but people usually just call them Beefeaters. Their nickname is thought to have come from the fact that the guards used to receive part of their pay in meat rations.**

⭐ Prisoners who were beheaded at the Tower actually had to pay for their own execution. It is not known whether the guards' favourite inmates were given a special discount!

⭐ **Honourable Londoners are sometimes offered the title 'Freeman'. One of the benefits of this position is the right to drive sheep over Tower Bridge. But we reckon you'd have to be *baaa*-king mad to try that!**

PLAN YOUR VISIT ⑨

Tower of London
Tower Hill, EC3N
www.hrp.org.uk/TowerOfLondon

📞 0844 482 7777

🕐 Tue-Sat (summer) 09.00-17.30
Sun-Mon (summer) 10.00-17.30
Closes at 16.30 out of season

⊖ Tower Hill

I want to go here ☐

GUIDE A WARSHIP'S GUNS

...on the HMS *Belfast*

Life on the HMS *Belfast* was a bit like being at a boys' boarding school – but without the maths lessons! There were about 950 men on the ship, but unlike boarding school there were big guns and even bigger battles.

HMS *Belfast* was launched in 1938, just in time to play an important role in World War Two. During the war she captured German ships and protected British convoys.

The *Belfast* was finally turned into a museum in 1971 and now you can explore all nine of her decks.

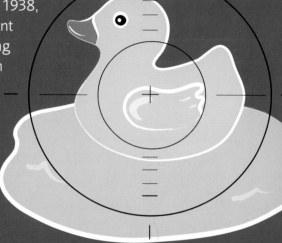

Sticker Scores

5 ADMIRAL OF THE FLEET

4 COMMODORE

3 COMMANDER

2 LIEUTENANT

1 STOWAWAY

Head to the gun turret on the ship's bow (the front) where you'll see real ammunition. Then climb up to the Gun Direction Platform at the top of the main tower and gawp at the ginormous guns. Look through the binoculars, take aim and (pretend to) fire!

Make A Day Of It

🗝 **Sleep on a pirate ship** at the *Golden Hinde*. This replica Tudor Galleon is moored near London Bridge and holds a sleepover once a month. You'll get to dress up as a pirate and sleep on the gun deck amongst the cannons – *arrr*-mazing! www.goldenhinde.com

Photo Op
Get a snap of you sitting in the Admiral's Bridge while pointing out to sea.

Fascinating Facts

★ **Being a crew member on the HMS *Belfast* was a risky business. The ship's doctors used 35.5 miles of bandages on sickly sailors between 1950 and 1952.**

★ The ship's powerful guns could blast their big bullets up to twelve and a half miles. If they were fired today they would reach as far as Heathrow Airport.

What's a Sea Monster's favourite food?
Fish and *ships*!

PLAN YOUR VISIT 🔟

HMS *Belfast*
Morgan's Lane, Tooley Street, SE1 2JH
www.iwm.org.uk

📞 0207 940 6300

🕐 **Daily (summer) 10.00–18.00**
Closes earlier out of season

⊖ London Bridge

£ ✕ 🎁

I want to go here ☐

The Murderous HMS Belfast

STARE A T.REX IN THE EYE

...at the Natural History Museum

The Natural History Museum's vast collection of stuffed animals, skeletons, creepy-crawlies and fossils is heaven for eco-enthusiasts. But the museum's star attraction is its terrifying tyrannosaurus rex.

Yes, we know dinosaurs have been extinct for ages. But the Natural History Museum has brought them back to life – sort of – by creating a moving model of a T.rex. Clever technology allows it to watch you as you dodge round the room.

It also has a disturbing habit of roaring, before fixing you with a menacing stare, as if deciding whether you would make a tasty lunchtime snack. We dare you to stare back!

Sticker Scores

5 TERRIFYING TYRANNOSAURUS

4 TOUGH TRICERATOPS

3 DECENT DIPLODOCUS

2 MEASLY MAMMAL

1 PATHETIC PLANT

What do you get when dinosaurs crash their cars?
Tyrannosaurus Wrecks!

Best of the Rest

 Don't miss the life-sized model of the biggest animal ever, the Blue Whale. Its heart is the size of a small car (but less likely to get you to school on time!).

Make A Day Of It

 Design your own coat of arms, using the clever computer at the Victoria and Albert Museum. You can also admire high fashion from throughout the ages in the Fashion Galleries and see some seriously sparkly stuff in the Jewellery Gallery. www.vam.ac.uk

Fascinating Facts

★ **Dinosaurs became extinct approximately 65 million years ago. There are lots of theories as to what killed them – a big famine, disease, broccoli – but no one knows for sure. Most people believe a massive meteor hit the earth and caused lots of dust to fly up. This stopped the plants from growing, so there was no food and everything died.**

★ The Argentinosaurus was one of the largest animals of all time, weighing up to 100 tonnes. That's the same as a Boeing 757 aeroplane (though less useful when heading off on holiday!)

PLAN YOUR VISIT ⑪

Natural History Museum
Cromwell Road, SW7 5BD
www.nhm.ac.uk

📞 **020 7942 5000**

🕐 **Daily 10.00-17.50**

⊖ **South Kensington**

FREE 🍴 🎁 ☂

I want to go here ☐

SWIM WITH SWANS

...at Hyde Park Lido

Some indoor pools have **c**ool stuff, like slick slides and fabulous flumes. But at this outstanding outdoor pool you can actually swim alongside swans. That's *swan* thing you won't find at your local baths!

Lidos are open-air swimming pools. In the 1930s people were dead keen on swimming, so they built lidos all across London.

The Serpentine Lido is particularly special as it's a fenced-off part of a large lake. That means you share the water with ducks and fish, as well as the swans.

But don't worry if you prefer to avoid animals when swimming – there's also a pleasant paddling area just for kids.

Sticker Scores

5	4	3
OLYMPIC SWIMMER	COMMONWEALTH CONTENDER	LOCAL LEGEND
2	1	
SCHOOL STAR	SWIFTLY SINKING	

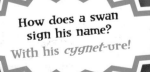

How does a swan sign his name?
With his *cygnet*-ure!

Best of the Rest

🔑 Hire a rowing boat on the Serpentine.

🔑 See the park on horseback by taking a lesson with Hyde Park Stables. www.hydeparkstables.com

Similar Spots

🔑 Kensington Gardens lies just to the west of Hyde Park. It's home to the Princess Diana Playground, which we think is one of the best in the city. There's a gigantic pirate ship to play on, plus a jungle gym, swings, slides and roundabouts. www.royalparks. gov.uk/Kensington-Gardens

You can go boating on the pond in Battersea Park during the summer months. There's also a zoo, adventure playground and subtropical gardens. www.batterseapark.org

Fascinating Facts

⭐ **During the 1100s, the king decided that the royal family owned all the swans in Britain. That's still the case today.**

⭐ It's been against the law to kill swans in Britain for hundreds of years. The law says that swan-assassins can be fined or even sent to jail. Apart from the fact it's illegal, it isn't very nice for the birds.

⭐ **Swans can fly at speeds of up to 60mph. That's about the same speed as a car driving along a motorway. We presume they don't stop at any service stations along the way!**

PLAN YOUR VISIT 12

Serpentine Lido
Hyde Park, W2 2UH
www.royalparks.org.uk
📞 **0207 706 3422**
🕐 **Daily (summer) 10.00-18.00**
⊖ **Knightsbridge / Lancaster Gate**
£

I want to go here ☐

SWAN LAKE!

GET IN A SPIN

...at the Science Museum

Have you got what it takes to perform the perfect spin? Well, you can find out at the Science Museum by having a go on this *revolution*-ary exhibit!

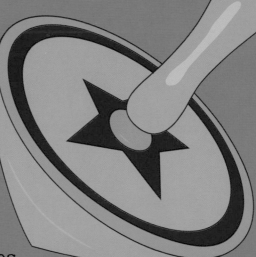

Rotation Station is one of many activities in the Science Museum's Launchpad area. Climb on board and start spinning with your bum sticking out. Then start straightening up and you'll notice how you suddenly pick up speed. This is the same technique used by ice skaters, some of whom can reach a dizzying 400 rotations per minute!

Sticker Scores

5	4	3
RIP-ROARING ROTATION	RAPID REVOLUTION	STANDARD SPIN

2	1
WEAK WHIRL	TERRIBLE TURN

Look out for other great experiments in Launchpad, including a giant wall of bubbles and a thermal imaging camera which shows you which parts of your body are the hottest.

Best of the Rest

 Power a lightbulb in Pedal Power (also in Launchpad). Use the pedals and hand-cranks to generate enough electricity to power up objects including a light, a hairdryer and a TV.

Make A Day Of It

 Taste the world's best cupcake at the Hummingbird Bakery. Our favourite is the Red Velvet – a red-coloured cocoa cake with a cream cheese topping. *Mmmm!*
www.hummingbirdbakery.com

 Conquer the climbing wall in Holland Park's adventure playground. The park also has a paddock with peacocks, as well as a cricket pitch, tennis courts and a beautiful Japanese garden.
www.rbkc.gov.uk

Fascinating Facts

★ **Ever wondered why you feel dizzy after you've stopped spinning? It's all to do with your body's balancing system. When you whirl around, fluid in your inner ear moves about and this tells your brain that you're in motion. The fluid continues to move once you've come to a stop, so your body is tricked into thinking that it's still rotating. This is what makes your head spin!**

★ In March 2011, a man in Pakistan spun a frying pan on his finger for a record-breaking 34 minutes and 30 seconds. What a stu-*pan*-dous performance!

PLAN YOUR VISIT (13)

The Science Museum
Exhibition Road, South Kensington, SW7 2DD
www.sciencemuseum.org.uk

📞 0870 870 4868

🕐 **Daily 10.00-18.00**
Closes at 19.00 during school holidays

⊖ South Kensington

FREE

I want to go here ☐

SHOP 'TIL YOU DROP

...at Westfield Stratford City

Westfield Stratford City isn't the sort of place you go just to pick up a pint of milk. It's London's largest shopping centre, and it's a pretty impressive place.

Opened in 2011, Westfield Stratford City is a shiny new shopping centre located next to London's Olympic Park. With 300 stores inside its doors, it's like an all-weather city!

But shops aren't the only thing you'll find at this mega mall. There's also a seventeen-screen cinema showing the latest movies and a 1950s-themed bowling alley called All Star Lanes.

Sticker Scores

5 — ENTHRALLING MALL
4 — SUPER CENTRE
3 — STANDARD STORE
2 — BARGAIN BASEMENT
1 — SHUT UP SHOP

Start by scoring a strike on one of their fourteen lanes, then head to the restaurant for burgers, milkshakes and cakes. We reckon it'll *bowl* you over!

Similar Spots

Westfield →

🔑 Westfield London in Shepherd's Bush is another enormous centre with a similar mix of shops, restaurants and entertainment.

🔑 It's not a mall, but Oxford Street is one of the top clothes shopping destinations in Europe. Check out the huge Topshop, which has loads of high-fashion clothes. Then pop round the corner to trendy Carnaby Street.

🔑 Hamleys on Regent Street has been London's top toy shop for over 250 years. You don't have to buy anything – it's just as much fun to wander round and watch the toy demonstrations and magic shows.

🔑 Covent Garden is a great place to shop for souvenirs. Don't miss the central Covent Garden Piazza, where you'll see buskers and street performers wowing the crowds. www.coventgardenlondonuk.com

Why did the skeleton go to the shopping centre?
To get to the Body Shop!

Fascinating Facts

⭐ **40,000 tonnes of structural steel was used in the construction of Westfield. That's about the same weight as 62,500 Formula 1 cars (but less nippy around corners!).**

PLAN YOUR VISIT 14

Westfield Stratford City
Montfichet Road, Olympic Park, EC20
www.westfield.com/stratfordcity

🕐 **Mon-Fri 10.00-21.00**
   Sat 09.00-21.00
   Sun 11.00-17.00

* Unless you buy something!

I want to go here ☐

LOOK INTO A CAMERA OBSCURA

...at the Greenwich Royal Observatory

What is a camera obscura? Well, it's actually Latin for darkened room. And, strangely enough, that's exactly what it is!

Before modern cameras were invented, people discovered that if you made a small hole in the side of a dark building, a clear picture of what was going on outside appeared inside the room. And it moved in real time, like a television screen.

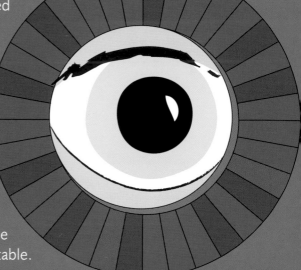

At the Greenwich Royal Observatory, the camera obscura projects the outside world onto a large circular table.

Sticker Scores

5	4	3
MOVIE MULTIPLEX	IMAX CINEMA	WIDESCREEN TELLY
2	1	
PANORAMIC PAINTING	SLOPPY SCRIBBLE	

It works best in bright weather, when you can spy on unsuspecting passers-by. Try and catch someone scratching their bum or picking their nose!

Best of the Rest

🔑 Steer a virtual ship at the National Maritime Museum. The ship simulator is in the Bridge Gallery and is similar to the machines used to train ship captains. There's also the All Hands Gallery, where you can load a cargo ship, send a semaphore signal and even fire a cannon! www.nmm.ac.uk

🔑 Also on site is the Peter Harrison Planetarium, the only planetarium in London. You can watch a show about space and the planets, plus see one of the world's most modern digital laser projectors.

🔑 Visit the observatory's enormous telescope. It's the largest one of its type in the UK and is over 100 years old. It sits in the building's curious onion-shaped roof.

The Peter Harrison Planetarium

Fascinating Facts

⭐ The observatory is also the site of the Greenwich Meridian – the line which divides the Earth into its east and west hemispheres. All distances and times on Earth are measured in relation to this point. At night a laser beam shines out from the observatory. This is partly to show where the meridian is, and partly just to amaze ya with a really big laser!

Photo Op
Take a picture of yourself standing in two different halves of the world, with one foot either side of the Greenwich Meridian.

PLAN YOUR VISIT 15

Royal Observatory
Blackheath Avenue, Greenwich, SE10 8XJ
www.nmm.ac.uk

📞 020 8858 4422

🕐 Daily (summer) 10.00-18.00
Daily (out of season) 10.00-17.00

🚇 Greenwich (DLR and rail)

£

I want to go here ☐

TAKE A TENNIS TOUR OF WIMBLEDON

...at Wimbledon Lawn Tennis Museum

In 1875, Major Walter Clopton Wingfield invented a new sport called 'Sphairistike'. The game was popular, but the name was ridiculous, so it was renamed tennis and people have been playing it ever since.

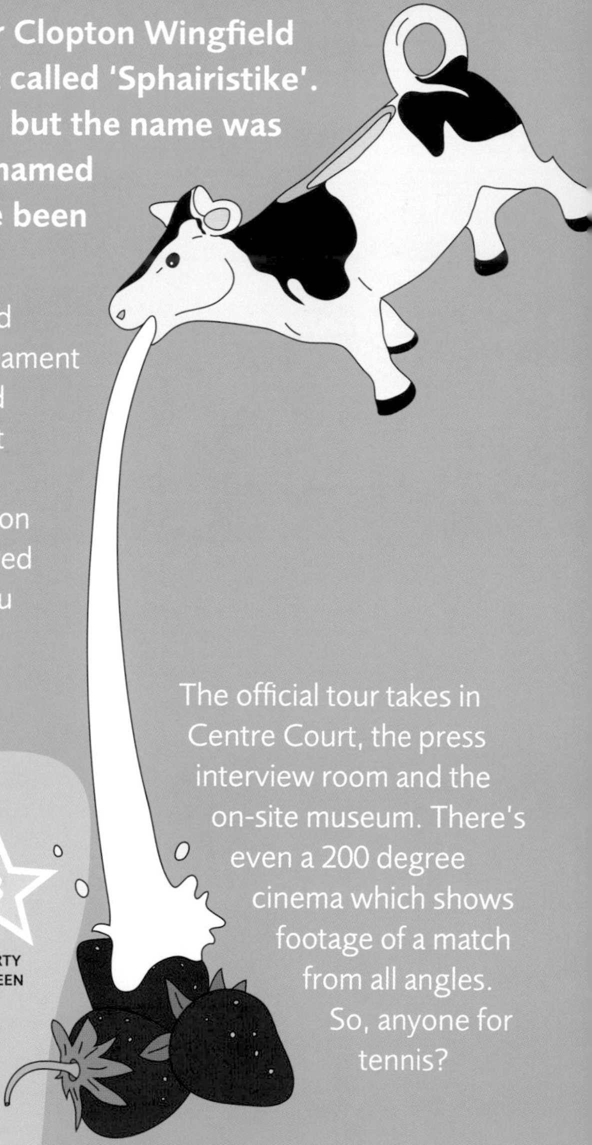

Wimbledon is the oldest and most important tennis tournament in the world. It was first held on a grass surface in 1877 at Major Clopton Wingfield's croquet club. The Wimbledon Championships are still played there in the summer, but you can visit at any time of year.

The official tour takes in Centre Court, the press interview room and the on-site museum. There's even a 200 degree cinema which shows footage of a match from all angles. So, anyone for tennis?

Sticker Scores

5 GAME, SET AND MATCH

4 FORTY LOVE

3 THIRTY FIFTEEN

2 LOVE ALL

1 LOVE NOBODY

Fascinating Facts

⭐ **Croatian player Ivo Karlović holds the record for the world's fastest serve. In 2011 he managed to biff the ball at 156 miles per hour. That's more than twice as fast as the UK motorway speed limit!**

⭐ Tennis was invented to be played on grass, which is why the organisation responsible for the game in the UK is called the Lawn Tennis Association. But these days Wimbledon is the only major tournament to be played on the green stuff. The others all take place on clay or hard court surfaces.

⭐ **When Wimbledon started it was just for men. However, a tournament for women was added in 1881.**

⭐ The first Ladies' Singles title was won by Maud Watson, who played against her older sister Lilian. They both wore white corsets and petticoats, starting a trend for nattily dressed tennis-playing sisters.

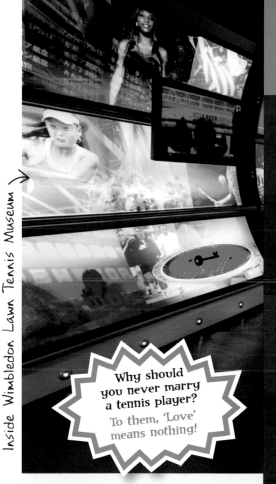

Inside Wimbledon Lawn Tennis Museum →

Why should you never marry a tennis player?
To them, 'Love' means nothing!

PLAN YOUR VISIT 16

Wimbledon Lawn Tennis Museum

All England Lawn Tennis and Croquet Club, Church Road, Wimbledon, SW19 5AE

www.wimbledon.org

📞 020 8946 6131

🕐 **Daily 10.00-17.00**
Closed during championships

⊖ Wimbledon

£££ ✗ 🎁

I want to go here ☐

Top Tip

Unless you have tickets for the tournament, make sure you don't plan to visit Wimbledon when the championships are taking place. They start in late June every year and last for two weeks. There are no tours during that period, and the museum is only open to spectators.

GET LOST IN AN ENORMOUS MAZE

...at Hampton Court Palace

Normally, getting lost is not to be recommended. But when you visit Hampton Court's world-famous maze, it's part of the fun. Just make sure you find your way out in time for dinner.

Hampton Court is the site of a grand old royal palace. It was built in 1514 for Cardinal Wolsey, who was a friend of Henry VIII (until Henry arrested him, anyway!). The maze was built about 175 years later, in 1690, and has barely changed since.

Sticker Scores

5 A-*MAZE*-ING MAZE

4 LEGENDARY LABYRINTH

3 PLEASING PUZZLE

2 RESPECTABLE RIDDLE

1 LOST CAUSE

Split your family into teams and race to reach the middle. Always stick with an adult – getting lost with a grown-up can be fun, but being stuck in a maze alone is not a great way to spend a day.

Photo Op
Have your photo taken at the centre of the maze, with your arms raised in a triumphant pose.

Fascinating Facts

⭐ The world's largest maze is the Pineapple Garden Maze in Oahu, Hawaii. It has a total path length of two and half miles and is made up of 14,000 colourful Hawaiian plants, including the pineapple. As far as we know, no one has ever tried eating their way out!

⭐ Studies have shown that laboratory rats find their way out of mazes more quickly if they hear classical music playing. We're not sure if Mozart will help you get out of the maze at Hampton Court, but we reckon it's worth a try!

Top Tip

During the summer you can get to Hampton Court by boat from Westminster. The boat service also stops at places like Kew and Richmond along the way.

Falconry at Hampton Court

What do you call a king that doesn't tell the truth?
The *lyin'* king!

Best of the Rest

🔑 Watch a falconry display. This is just one of the special events that take place at Hampton Court throughout the year. You can also catch Tudor cooking festivals, old etiquette lessons and even jousting classes!

PLAN YOUR VISIT 17

Hampton Court Palace
East Molesey, Surrey, KT8 9AU
www.hrp.org.uk/hamptoncourtpalace

📞 0844 482 7777

🕐 Daily (summer) 10.00-18.00
Daily (out of season) 10.00-16.30

🚆 Hampton Court

££

I want to go here ☐

WALK A TREE-TOP TRAIL

...at the Royal Botanic Gardens, Kew

Kew Gardens has thousands of trees, but from the ground you can only really see their trunks. So the best way to look at them in all their glory is to travel along the tree-top walkway.

Kew is home to the world's biggest collection of living plants. There are over 30,000 species in total, and 650 people are employed to look after them.

The tree-top walkway is the most exciting way to look round the gardens. It's eighteen metres off the ground (as tall as eighteen of you standing on each other's shoulders – just easier to walk along!).

Sticker Scores

5	4	3
TREE-MENDOUS	BLOOMING MARVELLOUS	*TREE*-SONABLE

2	1
OAK-AY	*YEW* MUST BE JOKING

After taking the stairs up to the walkway, snake through the trees while admiring the view. *Tree*-mendous!

Best of the Rest

🔑 Clamber across rope bridges and whizz along a zip wire in the Treehouse Towers play area.

🔑 Marvel at the insect-eating plants, prickly cacti and water lilies big enough to sit on in the Princess of Wales Conservatory.

Make A Day Of It

🔑 Go bird-watching at London Wetland Centre, a pretty and peaceful nature reserve on the banks of the river Thames.
www.wwt.org.uk

Fascinating Facts

★ **Trees are the oldest living things on Earth. The oldest ones discovered are a cluster of spruce trees in Sweden, which are around 8,000 years old and still going strong.**

★ The world's largest flower is the *Titan Arum*. It can grow up to three metres tall – the size of a small tree. It's also one of the smelliest plants, and it has the scent of rotting meat. This pong attracts insects that would normally feed on dead animals. That's a bit like wearing a poo-perfume to impress someone you fancy!

> What's black, highly dangerous and lives in a tree?
> A crow with a machine gun!

PLAN YOUR VISIT 18

Royal Botanic Gardens
Kew, Richmond, TW9 3AB
www.kew.org

📞 020 8332 5655

🕐 **Daily (summer) 09.30-18.30**
Closes earlier out of season

⊖ Kew Gardens

FREE

I want to go here ☐

TAKE A TUBE

If you've never been on a tube train before, you're in for a treat. The tube is basically a network of trains rushing through tunnels below London under the ground. That's right. UNDER. THE. GROUND. What's not to love?

Each tube tunnel is known as a line and has stops at regular points along the way. The first tube line opened in 1863 with open carriages running on coal power. All that fuel being burned made it stinky and smoky, so in 1890 they started to use electricity to run the trains instead.

All tube lines are fun the first time you use them, though the Jubilee's our favourite. It's the newest, and some of the stations have a funky, futuristic design.

Sticker Scores

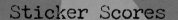

THE TUBE 5

YOU TUBE 4

TUBA 3

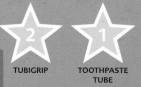

TUBIGRIP 2

TOOTHPASTE TUBE 1

Fascinating Facts

⭐ **The tube carries over four million passengers a day. That's more than the entire population of Wales.**

⭐ Angel station (part of the Northern line) has the longest escalator in Europe. In 2006 someone actually skied down it (and posted the video on YouTube). We really do not advise you to try this yourself.

⭐ **During World War Two, the tube was used as a shelter. People ate, slept and even gave birth in it.**

Make A Day Of It

🔑 Drive a tube train at the London Transport Museum. There are around 25 models on display, many of which you can get inside. Don't miss the tube train simulator, which lets you work the controls to move the train between stations. www.ltmuseum.co.uk

Comedy Drivers

🔑 Occasionally, tube drivers make funny announcements. Here are some of our favourites:

"Ladies and gentlemen, upon departing the train may I remind you to take your rubbish with you. Despite the fact that you are in something that is metal, fairly round, filthy and smells, this is a tube train and not a bin on wheels."

"Next time, you might find it easier to wait until the doors are open before trying to get on the train. The big slidey things are the doors, you can see by the way they open and shut."

PLAN YOUR VISIT 19

www.tfl.gov.uk

£

I want to do this ☐

HOP ON A ROUTEMASTER

No trip to London is complete without riding on a big red bus. And if you pick the right route, you can even take a trip on one of the classic Routemaster models.

London has a massive choice of bus routes, so you can use them to get just about anywhere. On most routes the traditional double-decker bus – known as the Routemaster – has been replaced by more modern designs. However it does still run every fifteen minutes on two special heritage routes. The number nine (which runs between the Royal Albert Hall and Aldwych) and the number fifteen (which runs between Trafalgar Square and Tower Hill) both feature Routemasters from 09.30 to 18.30.

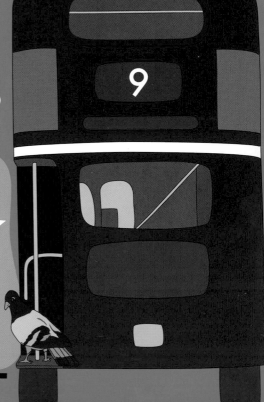

Sticker Scores

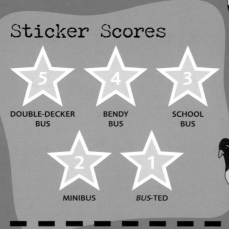

5	4	3
DOUBLE-DECKER BUS	BENDY BUS	SCHOOL BUS
2	1	
MINIBUS	*BUS*-TED	

Similar Spots

You can also ride through London on a duck! DUKWs are amphibious vehicles, which means that they can move on water and land. Hop (or waddle) on for an unforgettable look at some of London's most famous sights. www.londonducktours.co.uk

If buses don't *float your boat*, there are also river cruises and ferries which stop off at various points along the river Thames. Regular services are operated by TFL. www.tfl.gov.uk

Fascinating Facts

★ There are over 17,500 bus stops in London. 12,000 of these have shelters to protect customers from the rain. The other 5,500 are *not* great places to be in a storm.

★ More buses have been added to London's streets in the past decade. This means fewer people need to use cars, which is better for the environment. In 2006 there were more than 1.8 billion bus journeys around the capital.

What do you call a Spaniard whose vehicle has been stolen? Carlos!

PLAN YOUR VISIT 20

www.tfl.gov.uk

I want to do this ☐

RUN THROUGH THE PLAYERS' TUNNEL

...at Wembley Stadium

Wembley has been the home of English football since 1923. So if you plan on becoming a sporting superstar, there's no better place to get a taste of your future fame.

Wembley is not only a venue for major football matches. It also plays host to rugby league, American football and even the occasional pop concert.

On the Wembley tour you'll get to see the players' dressing rooms, the television interview room and the trophy winners' steps. There's also marvellous memorabilia, including the crossbar from England's 1966 World Cup win. But we reckon the best bit is running through the tunnel towards the pitch. Just think – the next time you visit, you might be taking part in a big game . . .

Sticker Scores

5	4	3
WORLD CUP	PREMIER LEAGUE	CHAMPIONSHIP

2	1
SUNDAY LEAGUE	MUCK UP

Why was Cinderella rubbish in goal?

Because she ran away from the ball!

Similar Spots

🔑 The Emirates Stadium is Arsenal's home ground. The club offers terrific tours – you can even upgrade to the Legends Tour and be guided around by an ex Arsenal star! www.arsenal.com

🔑 Chelsea play at Stamford Bridge in south-west London. Check the website for details of their access-all-area tours. You can even arrange a private one, just for your family and friends. www.chelseafc.com

Top Tip
Tours don't run on match days, so check in advance to see what's available.

Fascinating Facts

★ Wembley's striking arch can be seen right across London. It's 133 metres tall, which is the about same height as 12,000 chocolate bars stacked on top of each other (though less likely to melt in the sun).

★ The Jules Rimet Trophy (a replica of which you can see on the Wembley Tour) has had an eventful history. In March 1966, it was stolen from the museum where it was on display. A dog named Pickles sniffed it out a week later, and when England won the cup in July that year Pickles was invited to the celebration banquet to lick the plates clean!

PLAN YOUR VISIT 21

Wembley National Stadium
Wembley, HA9 0WS
www.wembleystadium.com

📞 0844 800 2755

🕐 Daily 10.00-18.00 (call to confirm)

🚉 Wembley Stadium

🚇 Wembley Park

£££

I want to do this ☐

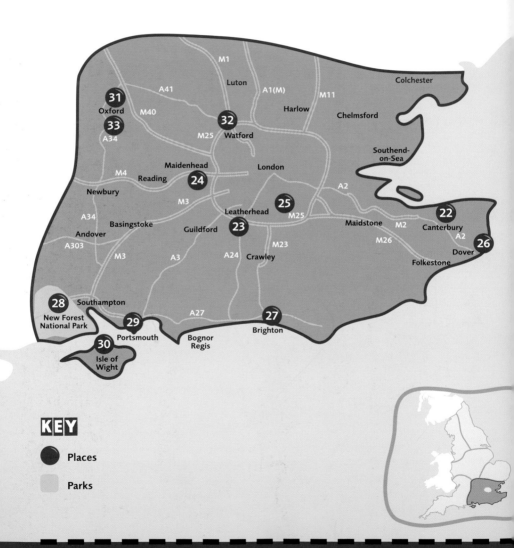

31 Oxford

33 A34

32 Watford

24 Maidenhead

23 Leatherhead / Guildford

25

22 Canterbury

26 Dover

28 New Forest National Park / Southampton

29 Portsmouth

30 Isle of Wight

27 Brighton

M1
Luton
A41
A1(M)
Harlow
M11
Colchester
Chelmsford
M40
M25
Reading
M4
Newbury
London
Southend-on-Sea
A2
M3
M25
Maidstone
M2
A2
M23
A34
Basingstoke
Andover
A303
Crawley
M26
Folkestone
M3
A3
A24
A27
Bognor Regis

KEY

Places

Parks

LONDON

SOUTH EAST

SOUTH WEST

EAST

MIDLANDS

NORTH EAST

NORTH WEST

TOP FIVES

RIDE A ROLLER-COASTER

...at Chessington World of Adventures

Everyone loves a roller-coaster, and this awesome adventure park is one of the best places to take the plunge.

Chessington World of Adventures is a theme park, an aquarium and a zoo all rolled into one. You can ride ripping roller-coasters in all kinds of themed lands (though some have height restrictions – see the website for more information). Alternatively, check out sharks and stingrays in the Sea Life Centre or come face to face with tigers, lions and gorillas in the Trail of the Kings.

Look out for the Wild Asia attraction, where you'll find the Kobra, a spinning disk ride that is shaped like a snake. Hold on tight or you'll be *hiss*-tory!

Sticker Scores

5	4	3
ROCKING ROLLER-COASTER	LUSCIOUS LOG FLUME	WHEELING WALTZER

2	1
HELTER SKELTER	DEPRESSED DONKEY

Top Tip

The restaurants get busier and the rides get quieter between 12.00 and 13.30. So if you have lunch either very early or very late you'll spend more time on the rides and less time in the queues.

Fascinating Facts

★ In 2007, a man from the USA broke the world record for the longest ride on a roller-coaster. He rode on the Big One at Blackpool Pleasure Beach for a staggering seventeen days!

Similar Spots

 Alton Towers (see p146) in Staffordshire is home to Oblivion, which is the world's first vertical drop coaster. Gulp! www. altontowers.com

 Drayton Manor Park, also in Staffordshire, has Shockwave – Europe's first ever standing-up roller-coaster. www.draytonmanor.co.uk

 The Pepsi Max Big One at Blackpool Pleasure Beach is a dizzying 65 metres in height, making it the tallest coaster in the UK! www.blackpoolpleasurebeach.com

 Lightwater Valley in North Yorkshire is home to the longest roller-coaster in Europe. The Ultimate is a whopping one and a half miles long! www.lightwatervalley.co.uk

Getting close to a meerkat at Chessington Zoo

PLAN YOUR VISIT 22

Chessington World of Adventures
Leatherhead Road, Chessington, KT9 2NE
www.chessington.com

📞 0871 282 5124

🕐 Daily (peak) 10.00-18.00
Opening times vary out of season

🚉 Chessington South

£££   ❗

I want to go here ☐

WATCH PIGS RACE

...at Bocketts Farm Park

Pigs might not fly, but what they *can* do is run. And there's no better place than Bocketts Farm to catch 'em in action!

The farm is home to all kinds of animals, including lambs, chickens and ponies. However, unlike most farms this one also holds a pig race twice a day! You can cheer on the heroic hogs as they race up the grassy hill to be rewarded with a tasty treat at the finish line.

And there's more to this place than watching pigs race. You can also pan for gold, take a pony ride or see goats being milked. We think it's an *udder*-ly fascinating farm!

Sticker Scores

5 GALLOPING GOAT

4 CANTERING COW

3 TROTTING TURKEY

2 LAZY LAMB

1 PLODDING PONY

Make A Day Of It

🔑 Go caving at Craggy Island Sutton. If you're eight years old or more, you can crawl your way through 50 metres of twisting tunnels. www.craggy-island.com

🔑 Create your own chocolates on one of the family workshops at Chocolart in Reigate. Dip marshmallows in the giant chocolate fountain to keep you going while you mould your masterpiece! www.chocolartltd.com

What do you get if you cross a pig with a dinosaur? Jurassic pork!

Fascinating Facts

⭐ Bocketts Farm has its very own *moo*-vie stars! Two of the farm's Jersey cows, Meryl and Beryl, are also retired actors who have appeared in the *Nanny McPhee* films.

⭐ *Boar*-lieve it or not, pigs actually have their very own Olympics! Events in the last championships included pig racing, pig swimming and even a version of football.

Best Of The Rest

🔑 Take a tractor ride. On a clear day you'll be able to see as far as the London Eye, over 20 miles away!

🔑 Ride the Astroslide in the indoor play barn.

PLAN YOUR VISIT 23
Bocketts Farm Park
Young Street, Fetcham, Leatherhead, KT22 9BS
www.bockettsfarm.co.uk
📞 01372 363764
🕐 Daily 10.00-17.30

££

I want to go here ☐

LOOK AT A LEGO LONDON

...at Legoland Windsor

Not all names describe a place accurately. For example, Greenland is covered in ice and Iceland actually has quite a few green bits. Thankfully Legoland is exactly what you'd expect – it's a theme park made of Lego!

Legoland has everything other theme parks have – rides, slides and attractions. The difference here is that almost everything is made of Lego. There are mini-brick buildings, and even Lego cars you can drive.

The most impressive Lego creation is Miniland, which contains model buildings from London and other cities. Look out for Lego landmarks like Big Ben, the London Eye and Tower Bridge (and to read about the real things go to pages 14, 18 and 27).

What do Lego men drive? *Brick*-up trucks!

TELEPHONE

Sticker Scores

5 LEGO LONDON

4 LEGO CAR

3 LEGO PYRAMID

2 LEGO VIKING

1 *LEGO OF MY LEG*

Make A Day Of It

🔑 Visit the Queen's favourite castle. Windsor Castle is the biggest and oldest lived-in castle in the world. Look out for the collection of armour which was once worn by kings, knights and princes. www.royalcollection.org.uk

🔑 Swing from a tree at Go Ape Bracknell. This terrific tree-top adventure course is located in the heart of Swinley Forest. Visitors must be over ten years old and weigh more than 45kg. www.goape.co.uk

Photo Op
Find your favourite mini-building and pose next to it for a snap.

Fascinating Facts

⭐ If all the Lego bricks ever made were divided between every living person, we'd all end up with 62 each.

⭐ It would take a tower of 40 billion Lego bricks to stretch to the moon. Sadly, we doubt that space rockets will be replaced by Lego stairs anytime soon!

Top Tip
There are sometimes large queues at Legoland, but you can avoid standing in line for each attraction by using the clever Q-Bot system. Details are on the website.

PLAN YOUR VISIT 24

Legoland Windsor
Winkfield Road, Windsor, SL4 4AY
www.legoland.co.uk

📞 0871 2222 001

🕐 Daily 10.00-18.00
Varies out of season

🚆 Windsor & Eton Central

£££

I want to go here ☐

FIND A GREEN MAN

...at Canterbury Cathedral

These green men wouldn't be much use when you're crossing the road. That's because we're talking about the stunning stone carvings you'll find in Canterbury Cathedral's cracking cloisters!

Canterbury has had a cathedral for around 1,400 years. The person in charge is known as the Archbishop, and the job also involves being head of the Church of England. The cathedral is a beautiful building, but its history is surprisingly bloody – four archbishops have been murdered over the years!

Our favourite part of the cathedral is the Great Cloister, which is filled with carvings of fascinating figures with funny faces and beards. Look out for the green men, who have leaves coming out of their ears and mouths.

Sticker Scores

⭐ 5 — CRACKING CARVING

⭐ 4 — AWESOME ETCHING

⭐ 3 — SOUND SCULPTURE

⭐ 2 — CHEAP CHISELLING

⭐ 1 — GRUESOME GRAFFITI

Best Of The Rest

🔑 Take the Tomb Trail. Look out for the tomb of Archbishop Chichele – it's on two levels and looks a bit like a bunk bed! Free trail leaflets are available from the Welcome Centre.

Make A Day Of It

🔑 Go rockpooling at Botany Bay, on the Kent coast. This quiet sandy stretch has perfect pools for spotting sea life such as starfish and crabs. Look out for cuttlefish eggs – they look like bunches of black grapes! www.visitthanet.co.uk

Fascinating Facts

⭐ **Thomas Becket was murdered after he fell out with King Henry II. However, clearly other people liked him, because a few years later the Pope made him a saint! Look out for the sword sculpture which marks the spot where he was slain.**

⭐ King Henry IV was buried at Canterbury Cathedral in 1413. When his tomb was opened 400 years later, his body was so well preserved that you could still see his ginger-coloured beard!

Top Tip
Visit the website and print off a voucher to get a free child's ticket (one per paying adult).

PLAN YOUR VISIT 25

Canterbury Cathedral

The Precincts, Canterbury, CT1 2EH

www.canterbury-cathedral.org

📞 01227 762862

🕐 Mon-Sat (summer) 09.00-17.30, Sun 12.30-14.30
Mon-Sat (out of season) 09.00-17.00, Sun 12.30-14.30
Parts may be closed to visitors at certain times.

££ ✖ 🎁

I want to go here ☐

WALK ALONG THE WHITE CLIFFS

...at the White Cliffs of Dover

These cliffs are more than just alright; they're also *all white!*

The White Cliffs of Dover are one of England's most famous sights and form part of its southern coastline. The cliff face is up to 107 metres high, and on a clear day you can see right across the English Channel to France.

Self-guided walks go from the Visitor Centre at Langdon Cliffs to the South Foreland Lighthouse – check at the gatehouse on your way in to find the best route for you.

Sticker Scores

5 CLIFFHANGER

4 ROCKING ROCKS

3 STANDARD STONES

2 SORRY SLATE

1 CLOTHES HANGER

Watch out for wildlife as you wander along – there are butterflies, wild flowers and even some grazing ponies. You'll be bowled *Dover* by the scenery!

Best Of The Rest

🔑 **Fly a kite** on the cliffs. Bring your own or grab one from the shop at the Visitor Centre.

Make A Day Of It

🔑 **Discover the secret wartime tunnels** at Dover Castle. This underground labyrinth was used by English soldiers during the wars with France in the 1800s, before becoming a military command centre during World War Two. www.english-heritage.org.uk

> **Top Tip**
> The cliff face is not fenced off, so make sure you keep away from the edge.

Fascinating Facts

⭐ **The cliffs are being worn away by the sea. This is a gradual process, but bigger bits can sometimes fall off in one go. In 2001, a chalky chunk the size of a football pitch crumbled into the English Channel!**

⭐ Not all of the most famous cliffs in England are 100 metres high and millions of years old. The singer Cliff Richard, for example, is under two metres tall and not much more than 70 years old.

> What do you call a man with a seagull on his head? *Cliff*!

PLAN YOUR VISIT ㉖

Langdon Cliffs
Upper Road, Dover, CT16 1HJ
www.nationaltrust.org.uk

📞 01304 202756

🕐 **Daily (summer) 10.00-17.00**
Daily (out of season) 11.00-16.00

FREE

I want to go here ☐

TAKE A GLASS-BOTTOMED BOAT TRIP

...at Sea Life Brighton

If you're fanatical about fish, you'll love the glass-bottomed boat ride at this ace aquarium. We think it's *trout*-standing!

Brighton Sea Life Centre is the oldest operating aquarium in the world. It's home to all kinds of aquatic creatures, from stealthy sharks to tropical turtles.

The glass-bottomed boat ride is a great oppor-*tuna*-ty to get up close to some fabulously fishy friends. You'll see colourful reef fish swimming beneath your feet as you sail across the ocean tank. It's a bit like snorkelling, but without getting wet!

We also like the jellyfish disco, where these wobbly wonders dance around in colourful tanks for your entertainment. It's great fun – and that's a-*fish-shoal*!

Sticker Scores

- **5** JAZZY JELLYFISH
- **4** GROOVY GOLDFISH
- **3** SWAYING SALMON
- **2** CLUNKY CUTTLEFISH
- **1** AWKWARD ANCHOVY

Best Of The Rest

🔑 Potter along the pier. Brighton Pier has an array of amusements, including a helter skelter and a carousel. Pick up a stick of sugary Brighton rock from the Candy Rock kiosk. www.brightonpier.co.uk

🔑 Peer at the pavilion. The Royal Pavilion is wonderfully wacky, both inside and out. Look out for the crystal chandelier that's held in the claws of a silvery dragon! www.brighton-hove-rpml.org.uk/RoyalPavilion

Fascinating Facts

⭐ The most poisonous jellyfish in the world is a form of box jellyfish known as the sea wasp. Each individual creature carries enough venom to kill 60 adult humans!

⭐ The largest animal that's ever lived is the Blue Whale. This colossal creature is the size of a jumbo jet and has a heart that's as heavy as a medium-sized car!

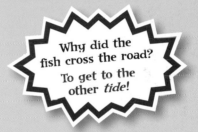

Why did the fish cross the road? To get to the other *tide!*

PLAN YOUR VISIT 27

Sea Life Brighton
Marine Parade, Brighton, BN2 1TB
www.visitsealife.com

📞 01273 604234

🕐 Daily from 10.00
Closing times vary

£££* 🍴 ☂

*Additional charge for the glass-bottomed boat ride

I want to go here ☐

RIDE A PONY

...in the New Forest

The New Forest is one of the prettiest parts of South East England. And there's no better way to see it than on four hooves!

The New Forest National Park covers over 200 square miles of land across Hampshire and Wiltshire, making it larger than the nearby Isle of Wight. The area's most famous residents are the 5,000 ponies who roam freely around the forest. We wish we had *neigh*-bours like these!

Choose from one of the many local stables for a perfect pony ride – options are listed on the New Forest website. And don't worry if you're not an expert; plenty of places offer beginners' lessons that will get you in the saddle in no time!

Sticker Scores

⭐ 5 — *MARE*-VELLOUS

⭐ 4 — PERFECT PONY

⭐ 3 — STURDY STALLION

⭐ 2 — HORRID HORSE

⭐ 1 — NIGHT-*MARE*

What do you give a poorly horse? Cough *stirrup*!

"Check out my mini-mohican!"

Fascinating Facts

⭐ **The New Forest isn't exactly new – it was first set aside as a hunting forest by William the Conqueror over 900 years ago. And although it's called a forest and still has wooded areas, many of the trees have been cleared over the years. However, we still think it's *tree*-rific!**

⭐ The New Forest ponies may roam freely, but they're not actually wild. They're owned by around 500 people known as commoners, who have an historic right to graze horses and other animals in the forest.

⭐ **The New Forest has its own pig patrol! The acorns which fall from the forest's trees in the autumn can be deadly to ponies and cattle, so every September a pack of pigs is sent in to gobble them up.**

Best Of The Rest

🔑 Have a stress-free cycle ride. The forest has over 100 miles of cycle routes through pretty villages and wonderful woodland.

🔑 Board a bus. You can hop on and off the New Forest Tour's open-top buses, which run regularly in the summer. www.thenewforesttour.info

PLAN YOUR VISIT 28

www.thenewforest.co.uk

FREE*

*Unless you're hiring a horse, of course!

I want to go here ☐

TRAVEL IN A MERLIN HELICOPTER

...at Portsmouth Historic Dockyard

Sadly there are no wizards involved, but we still think you'll have a *magical* time on the Merlin helicopter simulator!

Portsmouth Historic Dockyard is a working naval base with 800 years of history. It's the mooring place for maritime marvels like HMS *Warrior 1860* (the world's first warship powered by steam and sail) and HMS *Victory* (which Admiral Nelson fought and died on in the Battle of Trafalgar). You can still walk the decks of both ships today.

Sticker Scores

⭐ 5	⭐ 4	⭐ 3
HEROIC HELICOPTER	GREAT GLIDER	AVERAGE AIRCRAFT

⭐ 2	⭐ 1
POOR PARACHUTE	NOT ON YOUR *NELLY*-COPTER

The hands-on Action Stations experience features a full-scale replica of a Royal Navy Merlin helicopter. Climb into the cockpit and take the controls. Imagine you're on a military mission as you steer around an island before coming to land. It's a thoroughly *uplifting* experience!

what do you mean you've never flown one of these before?

Best Of The Rest

🔑 Tackle the tower in Action Stations – at 8.4 metres, it's the tallest indoor climbing wall in the UK!

🔑 Re-live a battle of the boats on the walk-through Battle of Trafalgar experience at the National Museum of the Royal Navy.

Make A Day Of It

🔑 Eat cake in the clouds at Spinnaker Tower in Portsmouth. Café in the Clouds is on deck two of this 170-metre-tall tower, which looks like a giant sail on the Portsmouth waterfront. You can also take the lift to the top and dare to 'walk on air' on the glass floor. www.spinnakertower.co.uk

Fascinating Facts

⭐ The Royal Navy has been using Merlin helicopters since 2000. They are 23 metres long and can fly at almost 200 miles per hour. It costs over £12 million to buy one, so sadly Santa is unlikely to be bringing you a Merlin this year.

Top Tip
Your ticket includes entry to six attractions (including Action Stations, two museums and the historic ships). So leave plenty of time for your trip!

Photo Op
Pose with the model of Henry VIII outside the Mary Rose Museum.

PLAN YOUR VISIT 29

Portsmouth Historic Dockyard
Victory Gate, HM Naval Base, Portsmouth, PO1 3LJ
www.historicdockyard.co.uk

📞 023 9283 9766

🕐 Daily (summer) 10.00-16.30
Daily (out of season) 10.00-17.30

£££

I want to go here ☐

TRY SAILING

...with Pelican Racing

Pelican Racing is located in Cowes on the Isle of Wight. The island is separated from the mainland by a stretch of water called the Solent, and you can get to Cowes by ferry from Southampton.

Pelican specialises in sports keel boats. These small yachts have heavy keels (pointy bits at the bottom of the boat), and so are unlikely to capsize. That's good news if you don't fancy falling in! Even beginners can try a Trysail. All equipment and training is included in the price, so just don some old shoes and get set for the *mari*-time of your life!

Sticker Scores

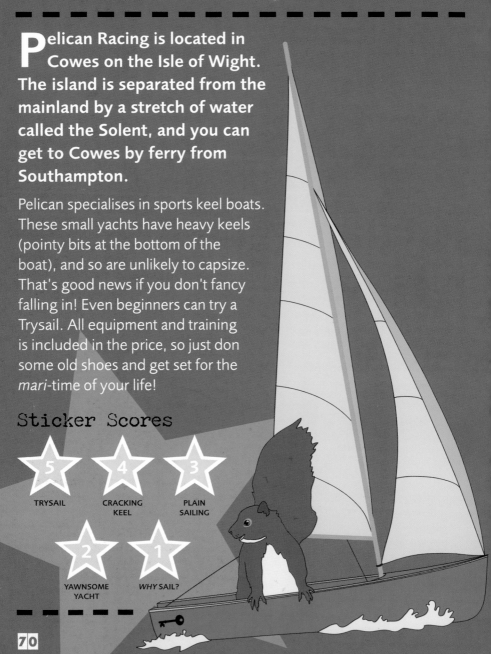

5 TRYSAIL

4 CRACKING KEEL

3 PLAIN SAILING

2 YAWNSOME YACHT

1 *WHY* SAIL?

Best Of The Rest

🔑 Spot a yacht in Cowes harbour. The highlight of the spectacular sailing season is Cowes Week in August – the largest sailing race of its kind in the world.

Make A Day Of It

🔑 Be dazzled by a dinosaur at Dinosaur Isle, which has a collection of fantastic fossils and prehistoric pieces. The dino-theme even extends to the building, which has been designed to look like a flying dinosaur! www.dinosaurisle.com

🔑 Build a sandcastle on Sandown Beach. This stretch of shore on the east of the island is a great place for a pleasant paddle or a delightful dip.

Fascinating Facts

⭐ **The Isle of Wight used to be a motorway for dinosaurs! Over 100 million years ago the island was joined to both England and France, so dinosaurs would travel across this strip of land as they migrated south.**

⭐ Over twenty species of dinosaur have been identified on the island, making it a dino-discoverer's delight. Visit Compton Bay on the west of the island at low tide and you can even see dinosaur footprints imprinted in the rock!

Photo Op
If the boat tips enough, try taking a picture of the keel. It looks like a dolphin swimming underwater!

PLAN YOUR VISIT 30

Pelican Racing
5 Birmingham Road, Cowes, PO31 7BH
www.pelican-racing.co.uk

📞 **01983 201581**

🕐 **Trysails can be arranged at any time – call ahead to book**

£££

I want to go here ☐

SEE A WITCH IN A BOTTLE

...at the Pitt Rivers Museum

There are lots of things that you'd expect to find in a bottle: fizzy drinks, medicine, and perhaps even the odd genie. But we've found something *witch* might just take you by surprise!

The Pitt Rivers is dedicated to anthropology – the study of human societies and their customs. There are around 100,000 items on display, from masks to musical instruments. There's even a piece of 100-year old cheese, made from Norwegian reindeer milk. It would be *rudolf* you not to take a look!

As for the imprisoned witch, no one has dared to open the silver bottle (sealed tightly with wax) since it was given to the museum in 1915. Apparently all sorts of bad things could happen if she were ever let out. So we suggest you leave your bottle opener at home!

Sticker Scores

5	4	3
BEWITCHING	WONDERFUL WITCH	*WITCHY*-WASHY

2	1
SAND*WITCH*	*WITCH*-FUL THINKING

Make A Day Of It

🔑 Grab an ice cream cone from George & Davies' café on Little Clarendon Street, just round the corner from the museum. www.gdcafe.com

🔑 Walk up a mysterious mound in the gardens of New College, one of Oxford University's 38 colleges. Climb to the top of the mound and clap your hands. You should hear a strange squeak echoing all around you. www.new.ox.ac.uk

🔑 Spot deer in Magdalen College's deer park (open afternoons only). And look out for gargoyles (grotesque stone carvings) lurking in the cloisters. www.magd.ox.ac.uk

Fascinating Facts

★ **During the Dark Ages, women who were thought to be witches were tortured and sometimes even killed. Some were set on fire or submerged in water to get the evil out of them.**

★ Pitt Rivers has some real shrunken heads on display! Some of these come from a part of South America where it was once customary to collect the heads of enemies killed in battle.

Best Of The Rest

🔑 Take the detective trail (you can download it from the website). Borrow a torch from the reception desk to light your way through the nooks and crannies!

Where does the witch send her children? To the day *scare* centre!

PLAN YOUR VISIT 31

Pitt Rivers Museum
South Parks Road, Oxford, OX1 3PP
www.prm.ox.ac.uk

📞 01865 270927

🕐 Tue-Sun 10.00-16.30
Bank holiday Mondays 12.00-16.30

FREE 🎁

I want to go here ☐

HANG OUT AT HOGWARTS

...on the Warner Bros Studio Tour

You don't have to travel from platform 9 and 3/4 to get to Hogwarts . . . just take the shuttle bus from Watford Junction station!

The Warner Bros. Studio Tour is a *magical* new attraction that lets you go behind the scenes of the sets from the Harry Potter movies. You get to peer into the potions classroom, hang out in Hagrid's hut and wander round the Weasleys' kitchen.

One of the highlights is the Great Hall. Follow in the footsteps of Ron and Harry, and look out for the graffiti that's been carved into the tables by cheeky students. Then pop into Dumbledore's office for a sneaky peek at the spellbinding sorting hat. It's never been so cool to *potter* around a school!

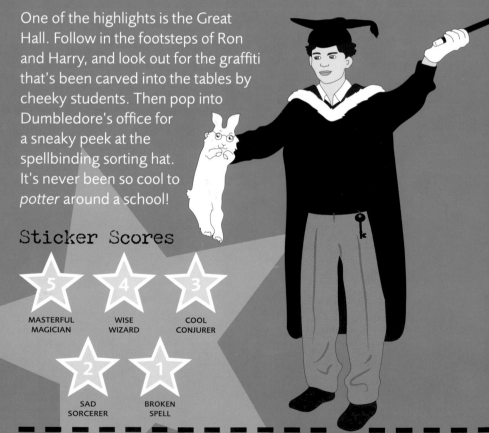

Sticker Scores

5 MASTERFUL MAGICIAN

4 WISE WIZARD

3 COOL CONJURER

2 SAD SORCERER

1 BROKEN SPELL

Best Of The Rest

 Discover the magic of green screen. This is the technological *wizardry* that was used to film amazing scenes like the quidditch matches. You can also admire Harry's Nimbus 2000 broomstick!

Similar Spots

 Hogwarts' Great Hall was modelled on the hall at Christ Church College in Oxford, and several scenes from the films were shot in the college's grounds. www.chch.ox.ac.uk

 Alnwick Castle in Northumberland was used to film the exterior shots of Hogwarts in the first two films. www.alnwickcastle.com

 Goathland station on the North Yorkshire Moors railway appears on film as Hogsmeade Station. www.nymr.co.uk

Fascinating Facts

★ The actors playing Harry and Ron outgrew their beds in the Gryffindor boys' dormitory over the course of filming the first Harry Potter movie. Some unique camera angles had to be used to hide the fact that they were now teenagers! You'll see the original beds from the film on your tour.

★ The Harry Potter books have been translated into more than 67 different languages and sold a *Ron*-believable 400 million copies!

Top Tip
Tours must be booked in advance, so phone ahead or go online to secure your place.

PLAN YOUR VISIT 32

Warner Bros. Studio Tour London
Aerodrome Way, Leavesden, WD25 7LS
www.wbstudiotour.co.uk

📞 08450 840 900

🕐 Tours start at 10.00

£££

I want to go here ☐

GET LOCKED UP

...at Oxford Castle Unlocked

Oxford Castle Unlocked sounds like something we might have written! But in this case we're not talking about a travel book – Oxford Castle Unlocked **is a guided tour around a fearsome fortress.**

Oxford Castle was used as a prison for nearly a thousand years. The last prisoners only moved out in 1996, so when you visit you'll get a real sense for what it was like to be locked up.

Costumed inmates guide you around and tell you terrible tales of prison life. Walk up the spiral staircase to the Saxon Tower and descend into the mysterious underground crypt, which is supposedly home to a host of ghosts. You'll even get locked into a cramped cell. Just hope your guide remembers where he put his keys!

Sticker Scores

5 JAILHOUSE ROCKS

4 IMPRESSIVE PRISON

3 STANDARD SLAMMER

2 CREEPY CLINK

1 LET ME OUT!

What did the executioner write with his pen and paper? A *chopping* list!

Best Of The Rest

 Be an executioner by pulling the lever in the Debtor's Tower. Be prepared for a blood-curdling creak!

Make A Day Of It

 Go punting from Cherwell Boat House. Punts are flat-bottomed boats that are propelled by poles. And they're perfect for pottering along the river.
www.cherwellboathouse.co.uk

 Play in the pleasure gardens of Blenheim Palace. There's an outdoor maze, a giant chessboard and wicked water gardens.
www.blenheimpalace.com

Fascinating Facts

★ **The last public hanging at Oxford Castle took place on the roof in 1863. However, executions took place in private for almost a hundred years after that. Hidden inside the prison walls is a secret room where prisoners were hanged right up until the 1950s.**

★ In 1850, a prisoner named Anne Greene managed to survive her own hanging at Oxford Castle! Afterwards it was decided that this was a miracle and so the lucky lady was allowed to walk free.

★ **If you thought being sent to your room was bad, spare a thought for the poor children imprisoned in Oxford Castle and forced to work for their dinner. The youngest inmate on record was just seven years old!**

PLAN YOUR VISIT 33

Oxford Castle Unlocked
44-46 Oxford Castle, New Road, Oxford, OX1 1AY
www.oxfordcastleunlocked.co.uk

📞 **01865 260666**

🕐 **Daily 10.30-17.30 (last tour at 16.20)**

£££

I want to go here ☐

Worcester

M5

A429

M50

Moreton-in-Marsh

Gloucester

42

43

Cirencester

41

Chepstow

A429

A40

34 **35**

Bristol

Bath

A350

Weston-super-Mare

A38

36 **37**

38

Warminster

40

39

Exmoor National Park

Barnstaple

M5

A37

A303

45

Taunton

Yeovil

A350

A361

Bude

A30

49

A39

A30

Exeter

44

Lyme Regis

A35

Weymouth

Poole

55

51 **50**

Dartmoor National Park

46

Newquay

Wadebridge

Plymouth

47

A30

52

A38

48

Dartmouth

St Austell

St Ives

Falmouth

53 **54**

Land's End

Lizard Point

KEY

● Places

▨ Parks

LONDON

SOUTH EAST

SOUTH WEST

EAST

MIDLANDS

NORTH EAST

NORTH WEST

TOP FIVES

SPLASH THIS WAY

SLIDE DOWN A ROCK

...on the Clifton Rock Slide

Most slides are made of plastic or metal. That's because plastic and metal are nice and slippery. Rock, on the other hand, is usually, well . . . rocky. However, this particular rock has been worn so smooth you can actually slide down it!

Close to the famous Clifton Suspension Bridge is an open limestone rock face with a slide running through the middle of it. Generations of kids (and quite a few adults) have zoomed down this rock, and each person's sliding bottom has helped to polish the stone into a slippery surface. It may not be quite as smooth as a normal slide, but where else do you get to slide on stone? In any case, we reckon it *rocks*!

> What is a stone's favourite music?
> *Rock* 'n' roll!

Sticker Scores

5	4	3
ROCK FACE	LOG FLUME	WATER CHUTE

2	1
SIMPLE SLIDE	BANANA SKIN

Make A Day Of It

🔑 Gaze into a gorge on Clifton Suspension Bridge. This dramatic structure is suspended above ground using massive chains. Stand on the pavement and stare into the swirling river below (this is safer than it sounds!). www.cliftonbridge.org.uk

🔑 Spy on passers-by in the Camera Obscura at the Clifton Observatory. You'll see live pictures of the outside world beamed onto the table in front of you.

🔑 Hand-feed the rainbow-coloured lorikeets at nearby Bristol Zoo. www.bristolzoo.org.uk

Fascinating Facts

⭐ People have lived close to the slide for thousands of years. Nearby Clifton Down is home to the remnants of an Iron Age hill fort. A Roman road also ran through the area. So it's possible that Roman bums helped to smooth the surface of the Clifton rock slide!

⭐ Limestone is not just for sliding on. It's also an important ingredient in cement, glass and even toothpaste.

Top Tip

It's best to ride the slide on a sunny day. Wear soft trousers, such as tracksuit bottoms, or just sit on a jumper instead.

PLAN YOUR VISIT 34

Clifton Rock Slide
Clifton Down, Nr Clifton Suspension Bridge

FREE

I want to go here ☐

SEE THROUGH YOUR OWN SKIN

...in At-Bristol

You don't have to be a ghost (or have super powers) to see through your own skin. Just use At-Bristol's vein viewer!

At-Bristol is an interactive science centre with the word 'at' in its name. ThAT's not something you see every day!

The vein viewer is in All About Us, which contains exhibits on the human body. A special camera shines near infra-red light onto the skin, capturing an image of your veins and arteries. Watch your blood moving as you clench and open your fist. We also love the camera that uses images to startle you and then captures your reaction on film. It's a real *shocker* – in a good way!

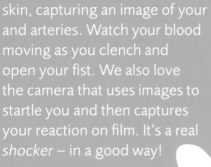

Sticker Scores

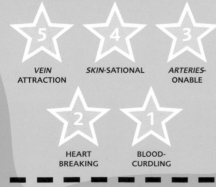

⭐ 5 — *VEIN* ATTRACTION

⭐ 4 — *SKIN*-SATIONAL

⭐ 3 — *ARTERIES*-ONABLE

⭐ 2 — HEART BREAKING

⭐ 1 — BLOOD-CURDLING

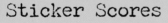

Best Of The Rest

 Explore more using the barcode on your wristband (which acts as your ticket to At-Bristol). Register the barcode online and you can access images from the startle camera and email them to your friends.

 See stars in the Planetarium – a huge dome lit up like the night sky!

Make A Day Of It

 Float on a boat on board one of the yellow and blue boats of the Bristol Ferry Boat Company. It's a *ferry* nice trip! www.bristolferry.com

 Bag a bacon butty from Brunel's Buttery on the harbour. It's a Bristol institution and well worth a visit.

Fascinating Facts

★ **Children have almost 100 more bones in their body than adults. These *bone*-us bits start to fuse together as you get older.**

★ There are around 60,000 miles of blood vessels in the human body. That means that if you stretched them out they'd go around world twice and there would still be some left over!

Top Tip
Look out for the four-metre high golden unicorns on top of the council building on nearby College Green. These mythological creatures feature on Bristol's coat of arms. You'll also see them on bridges and public buildings across the city.

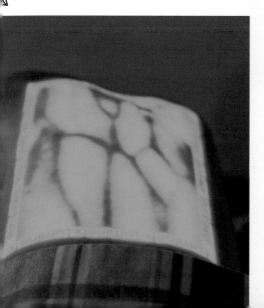

PLAN YOUR VISIT 35

At-Bristol

Anchor Road, Harbourside, BS1 5DB

www.at-bristol.org.uk

📞 0845 345 1235

🕐 **Mon-Fri (term time) 10.00-17.00**
Sat-Sun, holidays 10.00-18.00

£££

I want to go here ☐

MAKE A WISH IN A SACRED SPRING

...at the Roman Baths

Nowadays, baths are a dull (but necessary) part of the day. However, the Romans loved baths so much that the city is named after them!

The Roman Baths in Bath are heated by a natural hot spring which comes from deep within the Earth's crust. Romans believed that it was created by the ancient gods, so they built a temple here and used it as a sacred spot to bathe.

During your visit you'll see the impressive pools and also have a chance to throw a coin into one of them and make a wish. Just don't bother bringing a bath-time rubber ducky – you're not allowed in the water!

Sticker Scores

5 ROMAN BATH

4 WONDERFUL WATER

3 COOL POOL

2 SUPER SEA

1 MUD BATH

Make A Day Of It

 Find out about fashion at the nearby Fashion Museum. There's a huge range of clothes, shoes, hats and bags on display. Look out for the dressing-up section, where you can try on Victorian clothing.
www.museumofcostume.co.uk

Top Tip

Combine your visit with a trip to the Fashion Museum – it's cheaper to buy tickets for both at the same time.

Why did Julius Caesar buy crayons? He wanted to *Mark* Antony!

Fascinating Facts

★ When the water bubbles to the surface at the Roman Baths its temperature is 46 degrees centigrade. That's hotter than normal bath water (but less likely to contain bubble bath)!

★ The Romans built a temple at the baths to honour the goddess Sulis Minerva. People thought she would help against their enemies, so they threw curses into one of the pools on small pieces of lead. Many were written in code to make sure that only Minerva could read them.

★ Romans didn't just bathe in the baths – they also used them as a big social centre. People would play ball games, eat, drink and get massaged here. Think of them as a cross between a swimming pool, a gym, a pub and a football pitch!

PLAN YOUR VISIT 36

Roman Baths

Abbey Churchyard, Bath, BA1 1LZ
www.romanbaths.co.uk

📞 01225 477 785

🕐 Daily (peak) 09.00-22.00
Daily (out of season) 09.30-17.30
Times vary from month to month

££

I want to go here ☐

CLIMB UP A CLOCK TOWER

...at Bath Abbey

Usually you only look at clocks from the front, because otherwise it's a bit tricky to tell the time. At Bath Abbey, however, you can actually get in behind the clock face by climbing up the tower!

There has been an abbey here since 757 A.D., but the current church is actually the third building to occupy the site and was only completed in 1611. It's a pretty awesome construction and can hold up to 1,200 people.

We particularly like the tower tours. You'll stand on top of the abbey's ceiling, hear and see the church bells up close, and take in the amazing view from the top of the tower. You also get to sit right behind the massive clock face!

Sticker Scores

★ 5	★ 4	★ 3
BIG BEN	GRANDFATHER CLOCK	WRISTWATCH

★ 2	★ 1
STOPWATCH	STOPPED WATCH

Make A Day Of It

🔑 Watch glass-blowing at Bath Aqua Theatre of Glass. There are regular demonstrations throughout the day, and for an extra fee you can even have a go at blowing a glass bubble yourself!
www.bathaquaglass.com

🔑 Play in a teepee at the American Museum in Britain. You can also see bearskins and moccasins and dress up like a cowboy – *yee haw*-some!
www.americanmuseum.org

What's brown and sounds like a bell? Dung!

Fascinating Facts

⭐ Tunes played by church bells are never allowed to have the same two notes in a row. That's because each bell needs time to stop vibrating before being bonged again.

⭐ The abbey's tenor bell weighs a whopping 1,688 kilogrammes. That's about the same weight as a medium-sized car (but less useful on a motorway!).

Top Tip

For an amusing excursion, take a Bizarre Bath tour. They leave at 20.00 from the Huntsman Inn on North Parade Passage (Daily March-October).

PLAN YOUR VISIT 37

Bath Abbey
12 Kingston Buildings, Bath, BA1 1LT
www.bathabbey.org

📞 01225 422 462

🕐 Mon-Sat (summer): tours half-hourly 10.00-16.00
Mon-Sat (winter): tours at 11.00, 12.00, 14.00
Tours dependent on other events

£ 🎁

I want to go here ☐

GO ON A CRYSTAL QUEST

...at Cheddar Caves

Despite the name, Cheddar Caves are not made out of cheese. In fact they are a network of seriously cool underground caves!

Start off in Cox's Cave, where you'll find marvellous mirror pools and curiously coloured stalagmites and stalactites. It also contains the Crystal Quest – a fantastic fantasy adventure where you can help rescue the crystal of light from the lord of darkness, passing elves, warriors and smoke-breathing dragons along the way.

After capturing the crystal, head to Gough's Cave to see a 13,000 year old drawing of a mammoth. You'll also find the UK's largest colony of endangered greater horseshoe bats . . . and some cheddar cheese. You'd *brie* mad not to visit!

Sticker Scores

5 CHEDDAR CHEESE

4 CHEESE ON TOAST

3 CHEESE AND PICKLE

2 CHEESE SLICE

1 *CHEESE*-D OFF

Make A Day Of It

🔑 Ski down a dry ski slope at Avon Ski and Action Centre. You can also try your hand at archery, rock climbing, mountainboarding and abseiling. Check the website for details and age restrictions. www.avonski.co.uk

🔑 Ride a donkey on the beach at Weston-super-Mare (about a 30 minute drive away). The beach is one of the longest and sandiest in England, so it's a super spot for sandcastle building!

Similar Spots

🔑 The spooky Wookey Hole Caves are set in the limestone rock of the Mendip Hills. They even have their own resident witch! www.wookey.co.uk

Fascinating Facts

⭐ The oldest complete human skeleton in Britain was found in Cheddar. He is known as Cheddar Man and is about 9,000 years old.

⭐ Cannibalism is thought to have been common amongst prehistoric humans. In the Museum of Prehistory you'll see the remains of people who appear to have been eaten. We'd rather chomp on a cheese sandwich!

⭐ Unsurprisingly, cheddar cheese was invented in Cheddar. Though most cheddar is now made elsewhere, some is still made locally and stored in the caves.

Which is the best cheese to hide a small horse in? *Mask-a-pony!*

PLAN YOUR VISIT 38

Cheddar Caves & Gorge

Cheddar, BS27 3QF

www.cheddarcaves.co.uk

📞 01934 742 343

🕐 Daily (summer) 10.00-17.30
Daily (out of season) 10.30-17.00

£££

I want to go here ☐

SOLVE THE MYSTERY OF THE MEGALITHS

...at Stonehenge

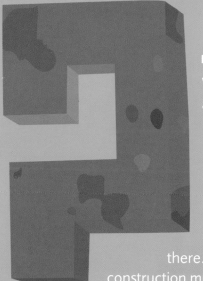

Normally, the idea of some stones in a field would not be that exciting. However, we're not talking about just any set of rocks. We're referring to Stonehenge's startling stone circle!

Stonehenge was probably built around 5,000 years ago, during the Stone Age. However, no one knows how the megaliths (large stones) got there. Each one is huge and very heavy, so construction must have been incredibly complicated.

The other big mystery is what the site was used for. There are all kinds of theories: some say it was a place for worshipping the sun; others believe it was used for healing or sacrifice. There's even a suggestion that Stonehenge was once a sacred graveyard. Maybe you can come up with your own theory!

Sticker Scores

⭐ 5 — STONEHENGE

⭐ 4 — STONE AGE

⭐ 3 — STONE STATUE

⭐ 2 — STONE COLD

⭐ 1 — STONE THE CROWS

Photo Op
Take a snap of you making a circle with your hands and standing in front of the famous stone circle!

Similar Spots

Stanton Drew Stone Circle near Bristol is a much smaller and quieter stone circle. It's free to visit and you can even have a picnic in the middle of the stones!

Make A Day Of It

See the tallest cathedral spire in Britain at Salisbury Cathedral. You can take a tour of the tower, which takes you right up to the base of the 123 metre high spire.
www.salisburycathedral.org.uk

Top Tip

You can book special Stone Circle Access visits which allow you to walk inside Stonehenge. They take place outside normal hours and need to be arranged at least a couple of weeks in advance.

Fascinating Facts

★ The megaliths at Stonehenge are partially buried in the ground to make sure they don't topple over. The holes were probably dug using antlers and bones, so it would have been back-breaking work.

★ Each megalith weighs between 20 and 50 tonnes. That's as heavy as 1,350 nine year olds!

★ Each year, hundreds of people spend the night at Stonehenge to celebrate the summer solstice. This is a festival to mark the longest day in the year, which some people consider to be an important spiritual event.

PLAN YOUR VISIT 39

Stonehenge
Nr Amesbury, SP4 7DE
www.english-heritage.org.uk

📞 0870 333 1181

🕐 Daily, times vary by month

££

I want to go here ☐

COME FACE TO FACE WITH A LION

...at Longleat Safari Park

Wiltshire is not the most obvious place to look at a lion. However, Longleat Safari Park is proof that you can get up close to one without going to Africa.

Longleat was the first safari park outside Africa, and it has been open since 1966. You drive your car through a series of parks filled with all sorts of animals you won't see at your average farm.

On your safari you trundle through Tiger Territory, wonder at Wolf Wood, gaze at giraffes and peer at pelicans. Our favourite bit is Lion Country, where the huge cats can come right up close to your car. Just don't get out to meet the lions, or you might end up as their lunch!

Sticker Scores

⭐ 5 — **LONGLEAT LION**

⭐ 4 — **GORGEOUS GIRAFFE**

⭐ 3 — **PRETTY PELICAN**

⭐ 2 — **WICKED WOLF**

⭐ 1 — **SCAREDY-CAT**

Best Of The Rest

Be batty about bats in the Animal Adventure section. If you're brave enough, you can stand in a room while bats fly freely around you!

Make A Day Of It

Drop down a death slide at Bowood House. Space Dive is a steep slide, which starts with a six-mctre vertical drop! There are also gorgeous gardens, an arboretum and a large lake to explore. www.bowood-house.co.uk

Top Tip

Check out Longleat's Junior Rangers videos in the KidZone part of their website. The rangers go behind the scenes at the safari park, handle snakes and feed sea lions.

Fascinating Facts

★ **A group of lions is known as a pride. Presumably lions are rather pleased with themselves!**

★ Female lions do most of the pride's hunting. The lazy males spend their time *lyin'* around!

★ **The giraffe is one of the fastest animals in the world, with a top speed of around 35 mph. That's faster than the speed limit on many Wiltshire roads!**

★ A tiger's stripes are as unique as a human fingerprint – no two patterns look the same. Even if you shaved off all a tiger's fur the stripes would still be visible on its skin.

PLAN YOUR VISIT 40

Longleat Safari Park
Warminster, BA12 7NW
www.longleat.co.uk

📞 **01985 844 4000**

🕐 **Opening hours vary – check website**

£££

I want to go here ☐

GO ON A CANOE SAFARI

...at Slimbridge Wildfowl and Wetlands Centre

We like feeding the ducks in the park, but we LOVE seeing all the different types of birds on a Slimbridge canoe safari. It's a wonder-*fowl* experience!

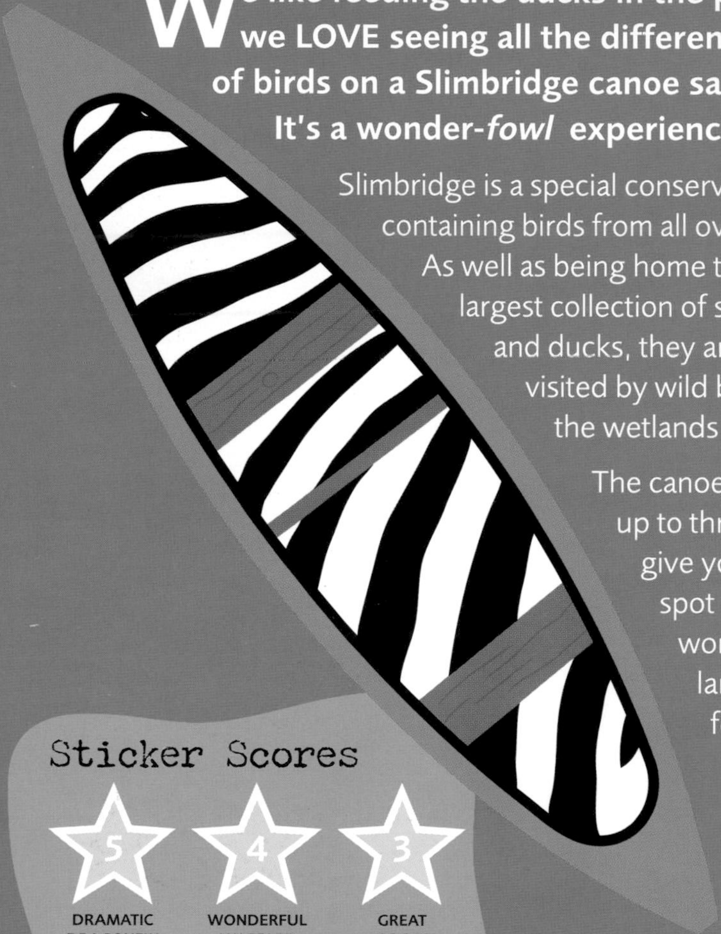

Slimbridge is a special conservation park containing birds from all over the place. As well as being home to the world's largest collection of swans, geese and ducks, they are also regularly visited by wild birds who love the wetlands setting.

The canoe safaris are for up to three people, and give you a chance to spot animals you won't see from dry land. Look out for water voles, dragonflies, warblers and ducks. You'd be *quackers* not to visit!

Sticker Scores

5 DRAMATIC DRAGONFLY

4 WONDERFUL WARBLER

3 GREAT GOOSE

2 DECENT DUCK

1 BIRD-BRAINED

What do you call a cat that has swallowed a duck?

A duck-filled fatty-puss!

Best Of The Rest

 Touch frogs, toads and newts at Toad Hall. There are regular talks where you get the chance to handle the amphibians.

Make A Day Of It

 Marvel at a medieval keep at Berkeley Castle. Don't miss the dungeon where King Edward II was imprisoned and murdered in 1327. www.berkeley-castle.com

 Play hide and seek in a tree museum at Westonbirt Arboretum. There are over 3,000 trees from across the world, including a lime tree that's 2,000 years old! Visit in the evening from late November to December to see the Arboretum transformed into an illuminated wonderland. www.forestry.gov.uk/westonbirt

Fascinating Facts

★ **Male ducks are called drakes and female ducks are known as hens. A group of ducks can be called a flock, a paddling or a raft.**

★ Slimbridge is particularly famous for the beautiful Bewick's swans which migrate there for the winter from arctic Russia. During the winter Slimbridge puts up floodlights so that you can see them eating on the lake.

Top Tip
Feed the ducks and geese with grain from the Slimbridge shop. Put the grain in the middle of your hand and hold it flat so they don't nip your fingers!

PLAN YOUR VISIT 41

Wildfowl & Wetlands Trust
Slimbridge, GL2 7BT
www.wwt.org.uk/visit-us/slimbridge

☏ 01453 891 900

🕐 Daily (summer) 09.30-17.30
Daily (out of season) 09.30-17.00

££

I want to go here ☐

BOTTLE-FEED A BABY ANIMAL

... at the Cotswold Farm Park

Here's a place where you can feed a kid without going near a human being. A kid is another word for a baby goat – and at the Cotswold Farm Park you can have a *go-at* feeding one yourself!

The Cotswold Farm Park is a working farm in the beautiful Cotswold countryside. It's home to *farm*-iliar favourites like sheep, goats, ponies and pigs.

Visit in spring to help out with bottle-feeding the baby lambs and kids. Feeding takes place twice a day in the Demo Barn. If you're lucky, you might even get to see a lamb being born! Later in the year you can see sheep shearing and cow milking demonstrations. There's even a wooden cow for practicing your own milking skills. It's *udder*-ly brilliant!

Sticker Scores

5 A-MOO-SING
4 BAA-MAZING
3 CROAK-AY
2 UN-*CLUCK*-Y
1 *BUZZ* OFF!

Best Of The Rest

🔑 Get up close to farmyard friends in the Touch Barn. You might even see a baby chick being born in the incubator!

🔑 Drive an electric tractor around the farmyard. There's also a giant jumping pillow and an awesome adventure playground.

Make A Day Of It

🔑 Find a flamingo at Birdland. This place has 500 birds, including fine flamingos, pretty pelicans and pleasant pheasants. Don't miss the penguin feeding, every afternoon at 14.30. www.birdland.co.uk

🔑 Get a giant's-eye view of the Miniature Village in Bourton-on-the Water. It's a mini-replica of the real village of Bourton, complete with shops, houses and even a model of the model village! www.theoldnewinn.co.uk

Fascinating Facts

⭐ **The Cotswolds are a range of hills that lie within the boundaries of six different counties – Gloucestershire, Oxfordshire, Somerset, Warwickshire, Wiltshire and Worcestershire.**

⭐ Look out for the Cotswold Lion lurking in the farm park! But don't worry, there's no danger of you ending up on the lunch menu! He's actually a very shaggy-looking sheep that's adapted to the windy weather.

Top Tip
Buy a bag of feed and you'll be able to feed some of the animals from your hand.

PLAN YOUR VISIT 42

Cotswold Farm Park
Guiting Power, nr Cheltenham, GL54 5UG
www.cotswoldfarmpark.co.uk
📞 01451 850307
🕐 Daily (Mar-Nov) 10.30-17.00

££

I want to go here ☐

PLAY HIDE AND SEEK

...at Puzzlewood

If you're a fan of hide and seek, Puzzlewood is the perfect place to play!

Puzzlewood is a giant natural maze in the beautiful Forest of Dean. The setting is so special that it's been used to film episodes of TV shows like *Dr Who* and *Merlin*.

Large limestone caves jut out of the ground and stone paths lead to secret dens and dastardly dead ends.

There are also wooden bridges and lookout points, so you can spy on your friends before jumping out and a-*maze*-ing them!

If it's raining, head to the indoor maze. There are seven secret objects hidden there – see if you can find them faster than your friends. Whatever the weather, we reckon you *wood* be mad to miss it!

Sticker Scores

5	4	3
PUZZLEWOOD	TANTALISING TREES	FINE FOREST

2	1
BORING BRANCHES	*WOOD*-N'T BOTHER

Make A Day Of It

 Take the sculpture trail from Beechenhurst Lodge. You'll see weird and wonderful structures along the way. Look out for a giant's chair made of wood and wire. www.forestofdean-sculpture.org.uk

 Search for stalactites – creepy hanging rock formations – at Clearwell Caves. If you're feeling adventurous, you can plunge below the surface on a semi-deep tour. This involves crawling and scrambling, so be prepared to get muddy! www.clearwellcaves.com

 Open up a massive lock at the National Waterways Museum in Gloucester. You can have a go at using a canal lock, have a boat race, or turn your hand to boat-building. www.nwm.org.uk

Fascinating Facts

★ The geological features at Puzzlewood are known as Scowles. These may sound like sulky faces, but they are in fact ancient limestone caves that have risen above the surface of the Earth over thousands of years. They are thought to be unique to the Forest of Dean.

★ The Forest of Dean was once an important mining area. Coal was dug up for fuel, iron ore was mined to make ships and trees were cut down for charcoal. The remains of mines can still be seen in some parts of the forest.

> Why can't a leopard hide? Because he'll always be spotted!

PLAN YOUR VISIT 43

Puzzlewood
Perrygrove Road, Coleford, GL16 8QB
www.puzzlewood.net

 01594 833187

 Opening times vary – check website for details

I want to go here ☐

RIDE ON THE TOP DECK OF A TRAM

...on the Seaton Tramway

In many parts of the world, trams are an important way for people to get from place to place. In Seaton, however, the trams are titchy and just for tourists!

The Seaton Tramway runs along a three-mile track from Seaton to Colyton, alongside the river Axe. All the fourteen trams that run on the line are mini-marvels with their own history and identity. Look out for car fourteen, which started life in 1904 as a working tram in London, or car eight, which is painted bright pink!

If the weather's good, take a seat on the top deck and keep an eye out for wildlife as you trundle along. You should see sheep, rabbits and all kinds of birds. It's a *tram*-endous way to spend a day!

Sticker Scores

5 TERRIFIC TRAM

4 TOP TRAIN

3 CRACKING COACH

2 BASIC BUS

1 BROKEN DOWN

Top Tip

Get an all-day ticket for unlimited travel. Use the spotters guide provided by the ticket office to tick off which trams you've ridden.

Make A Day Of It

🔑 Search for fossils along the Jurassic Coast, an amazing stretch of coastline running through East Devon and Dorset. Many of the coastal cliffs were formed during the Jurassic period up to 200 million years ago. Fossils can still be found on its beaches today – look for bits where the sea has washed away the soft clay and mud.

🔑 Explore an adventure park at Crealy. This ace place is packed with rides and slides and more besides. It's a 30 minute drive away from Seaton, but we reckon it's *crealy* worth the journey! www.crealy.co.uk

Fascinating Facts

★ In 2009 an enormous pliosaur skull was discovered on the Jurassic coast. The head alone measures over two metres – that's longer than most adult men! Pliosaurs lived 150 million years ago and are the largest sea reptiles that have ever existed. They could grow up to twelve metres long.

★ The Seaton tramway has a narrow-gauge track, which means it's thinner than normal trams or trains. The two rails are just 61 centimetres apart, whereas most trams run on rails that are at least 100 centimetres apart.

★ Many of the trams have cool reversible seats. You can move the seat forward or backwards to change the direction you're facing.

PLAN YOUR VISIT

Seaton Tramway

Seaton Terminus, Underfleet Car Park, Seaton, EX12 2TB

www.tram.co.uk

📞 01297 20375

🕐 Daily (Feb-Dec) timetables vary

££

I want to go here ☐

WATCH SHEEPDOGS HERD SHEEP

...at The Big Sheep

There's more to this place than bleating balls of fluff. They've got a farm, a play area and even a battlefield. We think you'd be *baaa*-king mad not to visit!

The Big Sheep is a a sheep-themed attraction – and we love it! You can see a sheep-shearing session, watch a sheepdog show and even cuddle sheepdog puppies!

What do you get if you cross a sheep and a kangaroo?

A woolly jumper!

Sticker Scores

5 LOVELY LAMB

4 MARVELLOUS MUTTON

3 GORGEOUS GOAT

2 STANDARD SHEEP

1 *LAMB*-ENTABLE

Away from the sheep you can ride a horse, take a tractor around the farm, pedal on go-karts and catapult water balloons at your family! We particularly like Battlefield Live, where you get to shoot lasers across a large open battlefield. So don't be *sheep*-ish – this is one place *ewe* won't want to miss!

Make A Day Of It

 Wield an ancient weapon at Torrington 1646, where costumed actors explain what life was like during the English Civil War. There are weaponry displays where you can learn how to use a pike (a long pole-like spear). You might even see a sword fight!
www.torrington-1646.co.uk

Photo Op
Have your photo taken before and after you go on Battlefield Live. We guarantee you'll be muddier in the 'after' photo!

Fascinating Facts

★ Candles were once made out of sheep's fat! Tallow (the proper name for sheep's blubber) has also been used as the basis for soap. However we definitely don't advise taking a leg of lamb into the shower!

★ Sheep have long tails when they are born. These are usually cut off when they are young to stop the tails getting clogged with sheep poo. Apparently sheep are not big fans of toilet paper!

★ The most famous sheep in the world is called Dolly. She was created in 1996 through a process called cloning. This means she was not born naturally, but grown by scientists using cells from another sheep.

PLAN YOUR VISIT 45
The Big Sheep
Abbotsham, EX39 5AP
www.thebigsheep.co.uk
📞 01237 472366
🕐 Daily (peak) 10.00-18.00
Sat-Sun (out of season) 10.00-17.00

£££ (peak) ££ (out of season)

I want to go here ☐

SPOT DARTMOOR PONIES

...on Dartmoor

Dartmoor is home to two famous populations: prisoners and ponies. You're unlikely to spot the inmates, as they're all (hopefully) housed inside Dartmoor prison. But anyway, we think the ponies are the *mane* attraction!

The Dartmoor pony has been around for 1,000 years. Despite its small size it's a very tough breed because it has had to get used to the unfriendly weather. These heroic horses used to carry tin across the moor from the nearby mines, and were even used in Dartmoor prison!

Sticker Scores

5 DIVINE DARTMOOR

4 EXCELLENT EXMOOR

3 AVERAGE ARABIAN

2 TIRED THOROUGHBRED

1 DEPRESSED DONKEY

When you're out walking on the moors you'll see small herds of ponies roaming about. Try looking around Widecombe-in-the-Moor, or Dartmeet. Wild horses couldn't drag us away!

What's black and white and eats like a horse? A zebra!

Make A Day Of It

🔑 Bottle-feed baby animals at Becky Falls – a wonderful woodland park next to a waterfall. www.beckyfalls.com

🔑 Climb up a tor (a local Dartmoor word for a hill) at Haytor. Haytor is 457 metres above sea level, so the views to the Teign Estuary below are *tor*-iffic. There's normally an ice-cream van at the bottom, so you can start your trek with a tasty treat! www.dartmoor-npa.gov.uk

🔑 See the Devil's Cauldron – a wonderful whirlpool at Lydford Gorge. You can also see the Whitelady Waterfall, where water plunges down a dramatic 30 metre drop. www.nationaltrust.org.uk

Fascinating Facts

⭐ **Each September, farmers get together and round up the ponies. This event is called a drift and is a big deal locally. People on bikes, horses and two feet round up the ponies then hand them over to their owners.**

⭐ Letterboxing is the name for a popular Dartmoor hobby. It involves searching for hundreds of hidden letterboxes using clues for their locations. Each letterbox has a stamp inside, so you can prove you've been there. Visit www.dartmoor-npa.gov.uk for more information.

Top Tip

Do not feed the ponies. It may seem friendly, but it encourages them to come close to the roads, and that can lead to them being killed by cars.

PLAN YOUR VISIT 46

Dartmoor
www.dartmoor-npa.gov.uk

FREE

I want to go here ☐

RACE CRABS

...at Dittisham

You don't need complicated kit to go crabbing. All you need is a long piece of string, some bait (we like bacon), a net and a bucket to put the crabs in.

Dittisham is a village with a pretty pontoon. Park at Greenway and take the passenger ferry across. If it isn't already waiting you can ring the bell and the ferry will come to fetch you.

Sit on the pontoon and lower your string (with bait attached) into the water until it hits the sea floor. Wait a few minutes then pull your line gently up to the surface.

Sticker Scores

5 — CUTE CRAB

4 — LOVELY LOBSTER

3 — PRETTY PRAWN

2 — COMMON CRAYFISH

1 — CRABBY PARENT

Hopefully a crab will be hanging on. We like to catch a couple and race them. See if you can guess which one will win!

Make A Day Of It

🔑 Feed a pelican at nearby Paignton Zoo. You can also catch feeding sessions with baboons, elephants and big cats. www.paigntonzoo.org.uk

🔑 Head to Blackpool Sands in Dartmouth. This beautiful beach is covered in shingle and therefore ideal for picnics as you won't get sand in your sandwiches!

Similar Spots

🔑 Teignmouth is home to a crab-tastic harbour with a colourful row of houses in the background. There's also a brilliant beach and a proper pier with super seaside entertainments.

🔑 Wembury (near Plymouth) has some fantastic rock pools, where you'll find all kinds of shellfish.

Fascinating Facts

⭐ If a crab loses a claw it grows back again. So if one drops off it's no *claws* for concern.

⭐ Walberswick in Suffolk holds the annual British Open Crabbing Championships. Only people who are born after 1890 are allowed to enter – but seeing as only one person has ever lived past the age of 120 this doesn't limit the field much!

Why do mussels and crabs never share anything? Because they're *shell*-fish!

PLAN YOUR VISIT 47

Greenway Quay
Greenway Road, Greenway, TQ5 0ES
www.greenwayferry.co.uk

📞 01803 882 811

🕐 Mon-Fri 08.00-18.00
Sat-Sun 09.00-18.00
Last ferry out of season is at 16.30

FREE (crabbing)   **£** (ferry)

I want to go here ☐

CLIMB A LIGHTHOUSE

...at Smeaton's Tower

Lighthouses are normally placed beside dangerous rocks so that ships can steer round them. So you might well wonder what Smeaton's Tower is doing on Plymouth Hoe, well away from the path of seafaring ships . . .

The answer is that Smeaton's Tower only arrived in its current location in 1877. Before then it stood at the treacherous Eddystone Rocks, fourteen miles out to sea. It was moved when the rocks beneath it were found to be unstable and has stood on the Hoe ever since.

Today you can climb all 93 steps to the top of the tower. Once there you have an amazing view out to the current Eddystone Lighthouse, which still stops ships being smashed on the rocks to this day.

Sticker Scores

5 LIGHTHOUSE   4 TREE HOUSE   3 WENDY HOUSE

2 GREENHOUSE   1 MADHOUSE

Make A Day Of It

🔑 Watch an octopus play at Plymouth's National Marine Aquarium. As well as the fascinating fish, we particularly like octopus playtime, when you can watch Bagpipe the octopus playing with a ball and other toys. www.national-aquarium.co.uk

🔑 See the Mayflower steps on the Barbican in Plymouth. The Mayflower Steps were the departure point for the Pilgrim Fathers who travelled to America in the 1600s and helped set up the country.

What type of building weighs the least? A *light*-house!

Fascinating Facts

⭐ The existing lighthouse was the fourth to be built on the site. The first two were destroyed by natural disasters and the foundations of the third can still be seen next to the lighthouse today.

⭐ One of the earliest lighthouses was the Pharos of Alexandria in Egypt, which was built between 280 and 247 B.C. It was one of the tallest buildings in the world at the time, and is now considered to be one of the Seven Wonders of the Ancient World.

Top Tip
Don't miss Britain's largest fireworks competition on the Hoe every August. It's a sparkling day out! www.britishfireworks.co.uk

PLAN YOUR VISIT 48

Smeaton's Tower
The Hoe, Plymouth, PL1 2NZ
www.plymouth.gov.uk
📞 01752 304774
🕐 Tue-Sat 10.00-12.00 & 13.00-15.00
£

I want to go here ☐

VISIT KING ARTHUR'S CASTLE

...at Tintagel Castle

Tintagel Castle is said to be the birthplace of King Arthur, the legendary British ruler. People disagree about whether he actually existed, but we can confirm that the castle's ruins are definitely real, and they're fit for a king!

The castle is perched on one of the most beautiful bits of Cornwall's rugged coast. It is accessible via a narrow bridge and steep steps – make your way down and imagine that you're at the centre of your own kingdom.

At low tide, you can also go down to Merlin's Cave, where King Arthur's magician advisor was supposed to have lived. But do be careful – the caves fill with water at high tide so check tide times before you visit.

Sticker Scores

5 KING OF THE CASTLE

4 BIG CASTLE

3 RUINED CASTLE

2 SAND CASTLE

1 CHESS CASTLE

Who built King Arthur's round table? *Sir* Cumference!

Make A Day Of It

🔑 **Wonder at a twenty-metre-high waterfall** at nearby St Nectan's Glen. You'll also see a money tree, which has coins hammered into its trunk!

🔑 **Get spooked** at the Museum of Witchcraft in nearby Boscastle. It claims to have the world's largest display of witchy items. www.museumofwitchcraft.com

Top Tip
Visit the English Heritage website and download the script for their family play about the castle. You can perform it together when you get there.

Fascinating Facts

⭐ **King Arthur was famous for ruling the royal court of Camelot. Camelot had a round table, with no official seat for the most important person, because Arthur and all his knights were considered equals.**

⭐ King Arthur was also the owner of a sensational sword called Excalibur. It was given to him by The Lady of the Lake, a mysterious water-dwelling woman. Sadly, all we've ever found in our local lake is lots of mud and the occasional crisp packet . . .

Photo Op
Strike a royal pose in front of the ruins.

PLAN YOUR VISIT 49

Tintagel Castle
Tintagel, PL34 0HE
www.english-heritage.org.uk

📞 01840 770328

🕐 Daily (peak) 10.00-18.00
Daily (out of season) 10.00-16.00

£

I want to go here ☐

CYCLE ON A CAMEL

...on the Camel Trail

Normally we wouldn't suggest you try cycling on a camel. They're too humpy and too hairy to make for a satisfying ride. Thankfully, the Camel Trail doesn't feature any actual camels – but it is one of the best cycle tracks in England!

The Camel Trail is the name for the stretch of disused railway line that runs between Padstow and Bodmin. Start your journey in Padstow, Wadebridge or Bodmin – there are bicycle hire points in each place. You'll pedal along pretty paths and through charming countryside. The full trail is eighteen miles long, but you don't have to cycle the whole thing. And if you want to share the workload, why not persuade a grown-up to join you on a tandem!

Sticker Scores

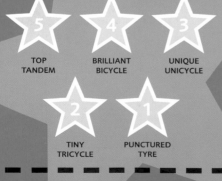

5	4	3
TOP TANDEM	BRILLIANT BICYCLE	UNIQUE UNICYCLE

2	1
TINY TRICYCLE	PUNCTURED TYRE

What is brown, has a hump and lives at the North Pole?
A lost camel!

Make A Day Of It

🔑 Walk the wobbly bridge at Lanhydrock's adventure playground, near Bodmin. There are also slides, climbing nets and monkey bars, all in the grounds of a cool country house. www.nationaltrust.org.uk

🔑 Pick your own fruit at Pencarrow House and Gardens, in Bodmin. www.pencarrow.co.uk

Similar Spots

🔑 The Tarka Trail in Devon is another brilliant biking route. It covers 30 miles of unspoilt countryside between the villages of Braunton and Meeth. www.devon.gov.uk/tarkatrail

Fascinating Facts

⭐ The trail is named after the river Camel, which runs alongside it. However, no camels ever lived nearby – the name comes from an old Cornish word meaning 'crooked'.

⭐ A camel is able to store energy in its humps, which means it can live without food in the desert for several months. Sadly, however, there is no food hidden along the Camel Trail, so we suggest you pack a picnic!

Top Tip

Download the Camel Trail leaflet from the website before you visit. It includes a map and some top tips on where to go along the way.

PLAN YOUR VISIT 50

The Camel Trail

Padstow to Bodmin
www.cornwall.gov.uk

📞 0300 1234 100

FREE (using the trail)

££ (hiring a bicycle)

I want to go here ☐

LEARN TO SURF

...at Harlyn Surf School

Learning to surf is not easy, but once you've ridden a wave you'll think it's well worth the effort. So if you think surfing's cool then you need to get yourself to a surf school!

Harlyn Bay is one of North Cornwall's nicest beaches. It's also a good place to learn to surf as its waves are relatively gentle. Harlyn Surf School offers a range of lessons: you can choose anything from a one-off family session to a five-day summer camp.

Alternatively, you can leave the board behind and take one of the Surf School's coasteering sessions. This superb sport involves jumping off rocks, exploring caves and wading through rock pools. Whatever you choose, we're sure you won't get *board*!

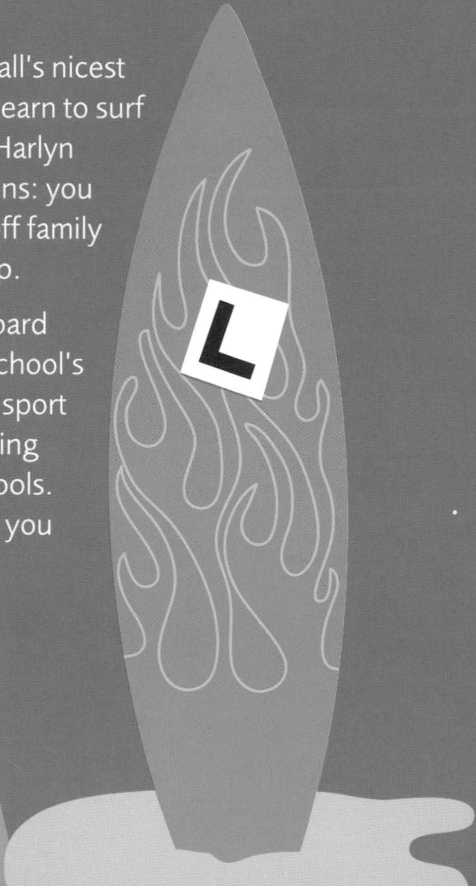

L

Sticker Scores

5 SUPER SURF

4 WONDERFUL WAVE

3 REASONABLE RIPPLE

2 SHALLOW SEA

1 *WAT-ER* DISAPOINTMENT

How do you say hello to the sea? *Wave!*

Make A Day Of It

 Go karting at St Eval Kart Circuit. There are several different kart sizes for kids aged seven and above. www.cornwallkarting.com

Similar Spots

 Gwithian Academy of Surfing has a Junior Surf Club for eight to sixteen year olds. The beach's gentle slope means that the surf forms and breaks quite slowly, so it's a great place for beginner boarders! www.surfacademy.co.uk

 Watergate Bay near Newquay is home to the Extreme Academy, where you can hire all kinds of kit including double bodyboards for two people! The academy also offers surfing lessons for those aged eight and over. www.watergatebay.co.uk

Fascinating Facts

★ **The largest wave ever surfed was over 21 metres high! The man on the board was called Pete Cabrinha and the wave was in Hawaii. It sounds pretty dangerous to us – we're not sure _Haw-aii_ did it!**

★ In 2005, 47 people managed to ride the same enormous surfboard in Snapper Rocks, Australia! Thankfully, at Harlyn Surf School they stick to one board per person . . .

Top Tip
Surfing and coasteering can both be dangerous without proper training and supervision, so we recommend you don't do either on your own.

PLAN YOUR VISIT 51

Harlyn Surf School
Harlyn Bay, Nr Padstow, PL28 8SB
www.harlynsurfschool.co.uk
 01841 533 076
Daily (peak) 09.30 & 13.30
£££

I want to go here ☐

RAMBLE THROUGH A RAINFOREST

...at the Eden Project

Cornwall may not be tropical, but that doesn't stop it from having its own rainforest. The incredible Eden Project is home to two dramatic domes, each with its own microclimate!

This amazing place contains peculiar plants and amazing animals from around the world. They live in biomes – ginormous greenhouses that look like bizarre bubbly mountains. One contains a Mediterranean landscape, while the other contains a re-created rainforest.

We particularly like the rainforest biome: you can see bananas growing on trees and walk around an indoor waterfall! Delve into the greenery or ride the rainforest balloon up to the top of the canopy (the bit among the tree tops). It's like a bit of Brazil has been plonked in the middle of Cornwall!

Sticker Scores

5 PERFECT PARADISE

4 GLORIOUS GARDEN

3 FANTASTIC FOREST

2 GRIMY GLADE

1 WOEFUL WOOD

Best Of The Rest

 Build a den! In the summer the Eden Project lays on activities for kids, including den building and storytelling.

Skate around an ice rink. Eden usually erects an awesome ice rink over Christmas – check the website for details.

Make A Day Of It

Take time out for tea at the Woods Café in picturesque Cardinham Woods. They offer chompable chocolate cake and cracking cream teas – a traditional treat that's particularly popular in Devon and Cornwall. www.woodscafecornwall.co.uk

Fascinating Facts

★ **The rainforest biome is a massive 240 metres long, 110 metres wide and 50 metres high. It's so big that you could fit about 15,000 London buses inside it!**

★ An area of rainforest the size of the Eden biome is destroyed on Earth every ten seconds. This is particularly worrying because the rainforest helps to slow down climate change.

What flower grows right under your nose? *Two*-lips!

PLAN YOUR VISIT 52

Eden Project
Bodelva, PL24 2SG
www.edenproject.com

📞 01726 811 911

🕐 Daily (peak) 09.30-18.00
Daily (out of season) 09.30-16.30
Late opening on selected summer evenings

£££

I want to go here ☐

GO TO THE END OF THE WORLD

...at Land's End

OK, so this might not be the end of the world, but it is the end point of the UK. Land's End is the most southwesterly point of the British mainland – and there's a sign to prove it!

Land's End is popular because of its position – people often cycle between here and John o'Groats, in Scotland, at the top of the country. There's plenty to do here – you can choose from a range of visitor attractions or alternatively take a walk along the wind-swept cliffs. While you're walking, look out for dolphins, porpoises and basking sharks. Whatever you do, just don't forget to stop at the car park, because if you carry on you'll run out of road!

World ends ahead

Sticker Scores

5	4	3
WORLD'S END	LAND'S END	CITY LIMITS

2	1
CUL-DE-SAC	DEAD END

Photo Op
Get a snap of you next to the famous Land's End signpost. For a fee you can choose to have a photo taken with the sign altered to point to your home town!

Make A Day Of It

🔑 Watch an outdoor play at the Minack Theatre, near Penzance. www.minack.com

🔑 Build a sandcastle on nearby Sennen Beach. This is a relatively quiet spot, with white sand that's perfect for creating castles.

🔑 Visit some silly islands. The Scilly Isles lie 30 miles off the coast from Land's End, and you can get there by helicopter, boat or plane. There are loads of things to do, from sampling sea sports to peering at puffins. www.simplyscilly.co.uk

Fascinating Facts

⭐ In 1968, the *Torrey Canyon* supertanker crashed into the Cornish coast between Land's End and the Scilly Isles. It spilled 31 million gallons of oil into the sea, causing an environmental disaster. Eventually it was bombed by the RAF to help break it up and set alight to the oil.

⭐ John o'Groats and Land's End are 603 miles apart. However, it takes at least 838 miles to travel between the two by road – so it's quite a trek for those who choose to make the journey!

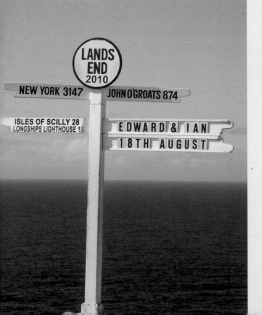

PLAN YOUR VISIT 53

Land's End
Sennen, TR19 7AA
www.landsend-landmark.co.uk

📞 0871 720 0044

🕐 Daily (summer) 10.00-17.00
Daily (off peak) 10.30-15.30
Late opening on selected August evenings

£ (parking)   ££ (attractions and parking)

🍴 🎁 ☂

I want to go here ☐

WALK THROUGH THE WAVES

...to St Michael's Mount

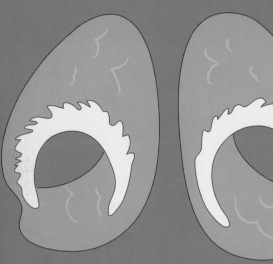

Normally we wouldn't recommend wandering through water. You're likely to get soggy, and there's always the risk of drowning. But at St Michael's Mount you can walk through the waves without getting wet!

St Michael's Mount is sometimes an island and sometimes part of the Cornish coast – it depends on the time of day! It is connected to the mainland by a causeway which you can walk along when the tide is low. It's like the waves have parted just for you!

Once you get to the island, check out the cool castle. We particularly like its gory defensive features – see if you can find the murder hole (a gap through which soldiers could attack their enemies) and the guns between the turrets.

Sticker Scores

5 MASSIVE MOUNT

4 HUGE HILL

3 STANDARD SLOPE

2 BORING BUMP

1 MEASLY MOUND

Top Tip

Try a Cornish pasty at the Phillips bakery in Marazion. Just don't munch it on the boat, unless you want to get seasick!

Make A Day Of It

🔑 Take a boat to the mount. When the tide is high, we definitely don't suggest you try to walk through the waves! Instead, take the boat from one of the landing points on Marazion beach.

🔑 Swim in an outdoor pool at the Jubilee Pool in Penzance. You can also admire the boats in nearby Penzance Harbour. www.jubileepool.co.uk

🔑 Descend into a tin mine at nearby Poldark Mine. A guided tour will take you through the tiny tunnels where children used to work during the 1700s. www.poldark-mine.co.uk

Fascinating Facts

⭐ These days the mount is home to the St Aubyn family. They've lived there since 1647 and plan to stick around for a while. Although they gave the mount to the National Trust in 1954, the agreement allows them to live there for the next 999 years!

⭐ St Michael's Mount is named after the Archangel Michael, who apparently appeared to fisherman there . . . But we think there's something *fishy* about that story!

⭐ Until a few hundred years ago, Cornwall had its own language. Penzance (close to St Michael's Mount) was one of the last Cornish-speaking strongholds. The last person known to have spoken only Cornish died in 1676.

PLAN YOUR VISIT 54

St Michael's Mount
www.stmichaelsmount.co.uk
www.marazion.co.uk for causeway timings

📞 01736 710507

🕐 Sun-Fri: causeway and ferry times vary

FREE (walking)　£ (boat)
£ (castle)　🍴 🎁

I want to go here ☐

ZOOM DOWN A FLUME

...at Splashdown, Poole

If you love whizzing down waterslides and zooming down flumes, this is one place where you're sure to have a *splash*-tastic time!

Splashdown is a wicked water park in the seaside town of Poole. Thrill-seekers will love the Screamer, which involves a dive down into a sheer vertical drop! Or if you're feeling fearless, try the Spacebowl, which spins you around before flushing you into a pool below. It's like being thrown down a giant toilet (but thankfully without the smell!).

We particularly like riding along on a rubber tyre on the Mississippi Drifter ride. Race against your friends as you're swept through pools and rapids. We guarantee you'll be *tyre*-d by home time!

SPLASH THIS WAY

Sticker Scores

5 *FLUM*-ING GREAT

4 SLICK SLIDE

3 PLEASANT POOL

2 FORGETTABLE FLUME

1 *WAT*-ER DISAPPOINTMENT

Why can elephants go swimming whenever they like?

They always have their trunks with them!

Make A Day Of It

🔑 Take a day trip to beautiful Brownsea Island. There are regular crossings from Poole Quay, and it's a great place to spot rare red squirrels. www.nationaltrust.org.uk

🔑 Swing over to Monkey World in Wareham. There are over 200 apes in this refuge for rescued primates. www.monkeyworld.org

Similar Spots

🔑 Splashdown Quaywest is located in South Devon. Try a thrill ride, or just relax in the pool and take in the stunning views over Tor Bay. www.splashdownwaterparks.co.uk

Top Tip
Splashdown's outside areas close during the winter, so check what's open if you're planning a trip out of season.

Fascinating Facts

⭐ The first man to swim the English Channel was Captain Matthew Webb, in 1875. It took him just under 22 hours, and he smeared himself in porpoise oil to keep warm. Sadly, Captain Webb's love of extreme swimming challenges proved fatal – he died eight years later while attempting to swim the rapids of Niagara Falls.

⭐ The biggest swimming pool in the world is in San Alfonso del Mar in the South American country of Chile. It's two thirds of a mile long and big enough to hold 6,000 standard swimming pools!

PLAN YOUR VISIT 55

Splashdown Poole
Tower Park, Poole, BH12 4NY
www.splashdownwaterparks.co.uk

📞 01202 716123

🕐 Opening times vary through the year – check website for details

££

I want to go here ☐

EAST

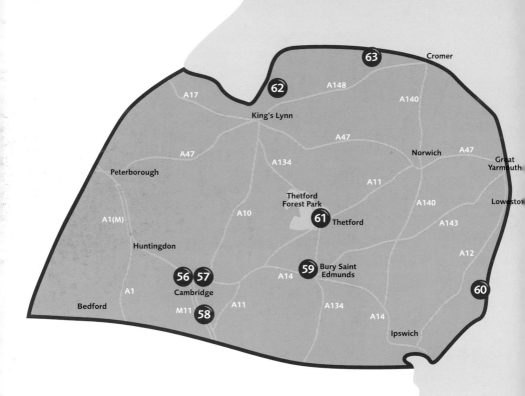

Cromer

63

62   A148

A140

King's Lynn

A17

A47

Norwich   A47

A47

A134

Great
Yarmouth

Peterborough

A11   Lowestoft

Thetford
Forest Park

A140

A10

A1(M)   61 Thetford

A143

Huntingdon

A12

56 57   59 Bury Saint
Edmunds

A1   A14

Cambridge

60

Bedford   M11 58   A11   A134

A14

Ipswich

KEY

 Places

 Parks

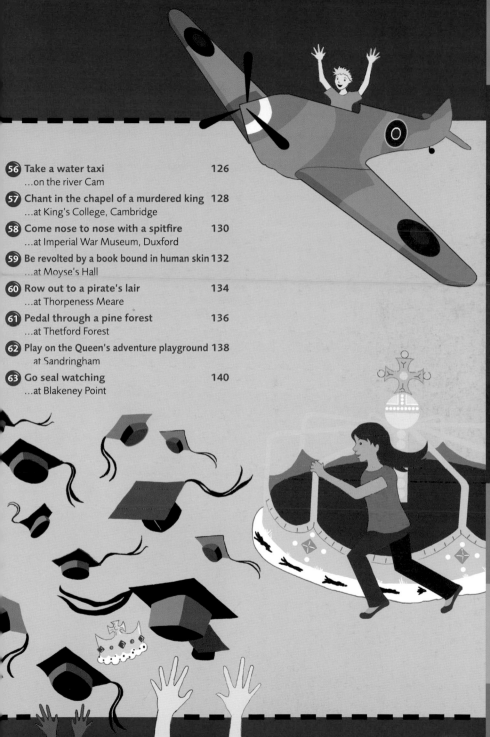

LONDON

SOUTH EAST

SOUTH WEST

EAST

MIDLANDS

NORTH EAST

NORTH WEST

TOP FIVES

TAKE A WATER TAXI

...on the river Cam

Taxis don't usually go along rivers. And taxi drivers don't usually wear straw hats. But both are traditional in Cambridge where you can be driven through the city on a punt!

A punt is a large flat-bottomed boat propelled by a pole. You can hire chauffeured or unchauffeured punts from several companies by the river Cam (Scudamore's is particularly popular).

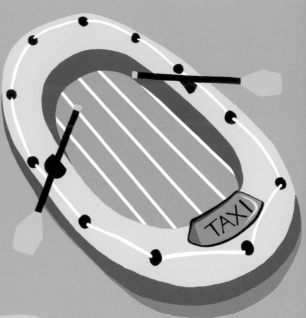

Punting is a great way to see the old university buildings and bridges. It's also much more difficult than it sounds – if you take an unchauffeured punt you'll need a strong grown-up with you. Just make sure they don't fall in . . .

Sticker Scores

5 POLE STAR	4 *OAR*-SOME	3 WORTH A PUNT
2 FLAT BOTTOMED	1 STUCK IN THE MUD	

Make A Day Of It

🔑 Scream at the world's largest spider at the Sedgwick Museum of Earth Sciences. The museum contains the fossil of the Megarachne, which crawled the Earth 300 million years ago. www.sedgwickmuseum.org

🔑 Pick up a tasty treat from Fitzbillies Bakery on Trumpington Street. Their Chelsea buns are particularly popular – and satisfyingly sticky! www.fitzbillies.co.uk

Top Tip
Cambridge has a muddy riverbed, so the punting pole can sometimes get stuck. If this happens to you then let go – it's better to lose your pole than end up in the water!

Fascinating Facts

⭐ Clare College bridge (which your punt will pass under) is decorated with fourteen stone balls. One has a missing wedge that looks like a piece cut out of a round cheese. Some people say this is because the bridge builder was not paid the full amount for his work and so removed a section in anger!

⭐ The fancy covered bridge by St John's College (known as the Bridge of Sighs) has been the site of some spectacular pranks. On two occasions cheeky students have dangled a car underneath it! We think that's *car*-azy!

What do you get if you cross a river and a stream? Wet!

PLAN YOUR VISIT 56

Scudamore's Punting Company
Granta Place, Mill Lane, Cambridge, CB2 1RS
www.scudamores.com

📞 01223 359750

🕐 Daily (summer) 09.00-21.00
Daily (out of season) 10.00-17.30

£££

I want to go here ☐

CHANT IN THE CHAPEL OF A MURDERED KIN

...at King's College, Cambridge

We all make excuses for not finishing things like homework or tidying up, but the man who started building King's College has a pretty good reason for not finishing the chapel – he was locked up in prison and then killed!

Construction of King's College's chapel was begun by King Henry VI in 1446. However, nine years after the first stone was laid, war broke out with a rival family over who should rule. Henry was imprisoned and killed in the Tower of London (see p26), so it was left to later kings to complete the magnificent structure.

Today, King's College chapel is home to a famous choir, which includes sixteen schoolboys from nearby King's College School. You can sing along with them at one of the term-time evensong services. It's an en-*chant*-ing experience!

Sticker Scores

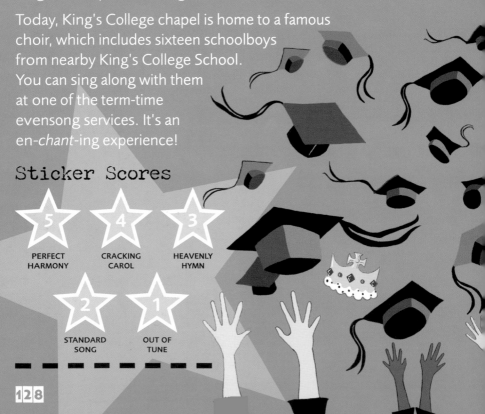

5 PERFECT HARMONY

4 CRACKING CAROL

3 HEAVENLY HYMN

2 STANDARD SONG

1 OUT OF TUNE

Best Of The Rest

🔑 Walk round a college. The city's famous university has 31 colleges and many are open to the public so you can walk around and see how the students live. We particularly like Magdalene and Trinity.

Make A Day Of It

🔑 Stargaze with astronomers, on one of the weekly space-observation evenings at the Institute of Astronomy. www.ast.cam.ac.uk

🔑 Peer at poisonous plants in the glasshouses at the Botanic Garden in Cambridge. www.botanic.cam.ac.uk

Top Tip
Combine a visit to the chapel with a stop at the **Fudge Kitchen** on King's Parade. They sell the finest fudge in the city!

Fascinating Facts

⭐ Henry VI was just nine months old when he became king. A group of advisors helped him govern until he was sixteen to make sure he didn't spend the royal budget on toys and sweets!

⭐ Henry came up with the rule that the chapel choir had to contain sixteen poor boys under the age of twelve who could read and sing. Sixteen choristers (choir boys) are still recruited each year. It's not compulsory to be poor any more though!

⭐ **Magdalene College is built on one side of a bend in the river. This was a deliberate design feature to separate the monks who used to study there from the temptations of the town on the other side!**

PLAN YOUR VISIT 57

King's College Chapel
King's Parade, Cambridge, CB2 1ST
www.kings.cam.ac.uk

📞 01223 331212

🕐 Mon-Sat (peak) 09.30-16.30,
Sun 10.00-17.00
Mon-Fri (out of season) 09.30 – 15.30
Sat 09.30-15.15, Sun 13.15-14.15
Evensong: Mon-Wed & Fri-Sat
(term-time) 17.30

FREE ☂

I want to go here ☐

COME NOSE TO NOSE WITH A SPITFIRE

...at Imperial War Museum Duxford

Despite its name, a Spitfire plane doesn't throw flames! In fact, these days the Spitfires at Duxford can't even fly . . . but they are great fun to visit!

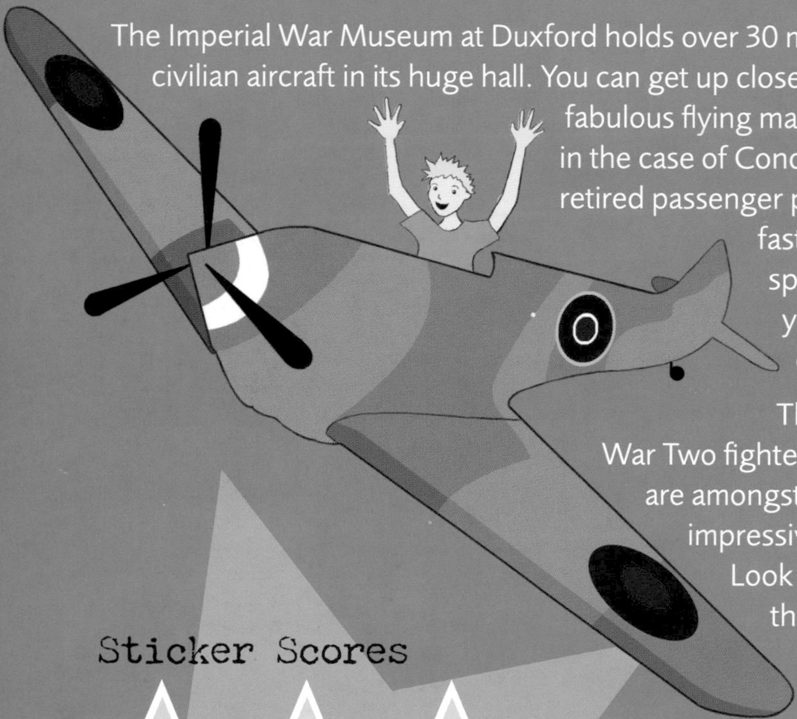

The Imperial War Museum at Duxford holds over 30 military and civilian aircraft in its huge hall. You can get up close to these fabulous flying machines, and in the case of Concorde (a now-retired passenger plane that flew faster than the speed of sound) you can even climb aboard!

The World War Two fighter planes are amongst the most impressive exhibits. Look underneath the marvellous Mosquito, and then admire the speedy Spitfires. If you're a fan of awesome aircraft you certainly won't be com-*plane*-ing!

Sticker Scores

5 FEARSOME FIGHTER

4 JUMBO JET

3 PROPELLER PLANE

2 GRACEFUL GLIDER

1 *PLANE* BORING

How do ghosts like to travel? By *scare*-oplane!

130

Make A Day Of It

🔑 Play croquet at Audley End. The flat lawns outside this smart stately home are the perfect place to play. www.english-heritage.org.uk

🔑 Feed rare farm animals at Wimpole Hall Home Farm. A Shire horse wagon takes you from the farm to the hall. There's also an awesome adventure playground made from old tractors! www.wimpole.org

🔑 Become an undercover agent at Spy Missions, an indoor activity centre that lets you take on the role of a spy. There are codes to crack, puzzles to solve and motion detectors to dodge! www.spymissions.co.uk

Fascinating Facts

⭐ The Spitfire was a British single-seat fighter plane that played an important role in World War Two. Some of the Spitfires were modified to carry small beer barrels under their wings instead of bombs. Troops on the continent were particularly happy when these planes arrived!

⭐ The aircraft hall at Duxford was built around the machines. This means that many of the larger planes – like Concorde – can never come out without demolishing the building!

EAST

Photo Op

The Duxford Airshow takes place in September. It's a rare chance to see historic and current RAF planes in full flight.

PLAN YOUR VISIT 58

Imperial War Museum Duxford

Duxford Airfield, Duxford, Cambridge, CB22 4QR

www.iwm.org.uk

📞 01223 835000

🕐 Daily (peak) 10.00-18.00
Daily (out of season) 10.00-16.00

££

I want to go here ☐

...at Moyse's Hall

A book's cover should give you an idea of what it is about. At Moyse's Hall you'll see an extreme example of this – a book describing a murder trial that's bound in the criminal's skin!

Moyse's Hall Museum contains artefacts connected with the Red Barn murder. In 1827, a woman called Maria Marten was shot dead by her lover William Corder. Her body was found in the Red Barn near Bury St Edmunds. Corder was tracked down, tried and hanged.

THE BELLY BUTTON BOOK

Sticker Scores

5 CREEPY COVER

4 BLOODTHIRSTY BINDING

3 JITTERY JACKET

2 TERRIBLE TOME

1 VILE VOLUME

When you visit, you'll see a report of the trial which has a cover made from Corder's skin! Also on display are Corder's scalp, ear and death mask (a wax cast of his face made shortly after death). It's a gruesome way to spend a day!

Best Of The Rest

Try brass rubbing. Materials are provided for you to create your own seal of St Edmund, the founder of Bury. (We mean a wax seal by the way – St Edmund was not a marine mammal!)

Make A Day Of It

Go on a backstage tour at the nineteenth century Theatre Royal, Bury St Edmunds. For the full experience, stay behind afterwards for one of the kids' shows. www.theatreroyal.org

Fascinating Facts

★ Maria's decomposing head was used as evidence in the trial, as the wounds to her skull showed that she had been shot.

★ The case captured the public's imagination, with thousands wanting to see the Red Barn for themselves. The rope used to hang Corder was cut into small sections and sold as souvenirs. We'd rather have a stick of rock!

★ Corder's skeleton was donated to West Suffolk Hospital. Until the 1940s, it was used to teach nurses about parts of the body. Sometimes they even took it to dances!

EAST

American Clocks

PLAN YOUR VISIT 59

Moyse's Hall Museum
Cornhill, Bury St Edmunds, IP33 1DX
www.stedmundsbury.gov.uk

📞 01284 757160

🕐 Daily 10.00-16.00

I want to go here ☐

ROW OUT TO A PIRATE'S LAIR

...at the Thorpeness Meare

You don't have to cross the Caribbean to reach a pirate's island! There are bays and coves a-plenty on the boating lake at Thorpeness.

Thorpeness is a remarkable holiday village that was built by a curious chap called Stuart Ogilvie. Stuart decided that the area was a perfect holiday destination . . . so in the early 1900s he built a bunch of houses, a lake (the Meare) and some tiny islands here. We reckon you'll be particularly impressed by the Pirate's Lair – because we *aaaarr*!!

There are many ways to look around the lake – you can rent rowing boats, canoes or pedalos. In our opinion, Thorpeness is a modern day *Meare*-acle!

Sticker Scores

5 SHIP SHAPE

4 ROCKING ROW BOAT

3 CANNY CANOE

2 DINGY DINGHY

1 PEDAL-0 DEAR!

Make A Day Of It

 Be amazed by the House in the Clouds, which overlooks the Thorpeness Meare. This architectural curiosity is a house built on top of a water tower. It looks like it's floating above the trees!

 Chomp on some cracking fish and chips at The Fish and Chip Shop on Aldeburgh High Street. We think they serve the best fish supper in the East of England!

 Potter along the pier in the scaside town of Southwold, which is a 30 minute drive away from Thorpeness Meare. The Under the Pier Show is full of wacky machines and simulator rides. www.underthepier.com

Fascinating Facts

★ Ogilvie was inspired to make a mystical holiday land by his friend J.M. Barrie – the author of *Peter Pan*. Many of the places at Thorpeness have names that refer to the book, like the Pirate's Lair and Wendy's Place.

★ **One of the most popular monuments in London is the Peter Pan statue in Kensington Gardens. It was put up secretly in the night on May 1st 1912 – so many people assumed it had appeared by magic!**

Why does Peter Pan always fly? Because he can *Neverland!*

PLAN YOUR VISIT 60

The Thorpeness Meare

Remembrance Road, Aldringham, Thorpeness, IP16 4NW

www.themeareatthorpeness.com

✆ 01728 832523

££

I want to go here ☐

PEDAL THROUGH A PINE FOREST

...at Thetford Forest

Thetford Forest is the largest lowland forest in the UK. It is also one of the driest spots in the country. And all this makes it perfect territory to go exploring on two wheels.

The forest is crisscrossed with walking and cycling tracks. There are four coloured biking routes; from the gentle green for beginners to the very difficult black trail. Bikes can be hired from Bike Art at the High Lodge Forest Centre.

On your ride you will pedal past pine trees and all types of wildlife. The forest is home to several species of deer and snakes, so be careful not to run them over – that would be a *wheely* bad idea!

Sticker Scores

⭐ 5 TOP GEAR	⭐ 4 PEDAL POWER	⭐ 3 PUMPED UP
⭐ 2 SLOW PUNCTURE	⭐ 1 ON YER BIKE	

Make A Day Of It

🔑 Feed the giraffes at Banham Zoo. Banham has loads of animals, and the large open plan design means they are well cared for.
www.banhamzoo.co.uk

🔑 Swing from tree to tree on the awesome Go Ape forest obstacle course, which is also in Thetford Forest. Age restrictions apply.

🔑 Go down a 5,000 year old flint mine at Grime's Graves. You descend nine metres down a ladder then walk to the viewing galleries to see the gleaming black flint.
www.english-heritage.org.uk

What do you call a bike with a degree?
A *uni*-cycle!

Fascinating Facts

⭐ The British Siberian Husky Racing Association sometimes holds events in the forest. Husky dogs pull along competitors, who stand on a sleigh with wheels. Sadly though, sleighs are not available for hire!

⭐ Thetford is overrun with rabbits. Warrens (huge rabbit homes) were set up by humans in the Middle Ages to breed rabbits that would provide food and fur. At the height of the industry there were up to 800,000 rabbits in the area – four times the human population of Thetford today! The number of rabbits has decreased since then, but you should still spot plenty hopping about.

PLAN YOUR VISIT 61

Bike Art
High Lodge Forest Centre, Thetford Forest, IP27 0AF
www.forestry.gov.uk/thetfordforestpark
📞 **01842 810090**
🕐 **Daily (summer) 09.00-18.00**
Daily (out of season) 09.00-16.00

££

I want to go here ☐

...at Sandringham

OK, we admit we haven't actually *seen* the Queen on the swings at Sandringham. But waving at crowds must get boring. And this adventure playground is basically in her back garden.

Sandringham is one of the royal family's country homes – they go there every Christmas. When they're away, the house is open to the public. Inside, you can see many fascinating royal objects, from exotic pearls to the clock used to time Her Majesty's racing pigeons.

Sticker Scores

5 PRINCE'S PLAYGROUND

4 KING'S SWING

3 QUEEN'S CLIMBING FRAME

2 MAID'S MERRY-GO-ROUND

1 PAUPER'S PLAYGROUND

The house is set amidst 60 acres of woodland. Follow the forest trails and then test out the awesome adventure playground. You'll have a right royal time!

LAYGROUND

Make A Day Of It

🔑 Bake your own bread at Bircham Windmill. The kids' cookery corner is in the bakery at the bottom of the windmill. It's a great place to test out your baking skills, and the mill owners will provide you with everything you *knead*!
www.birchamwindmill.co.uk

🔑 Support rescued sea life at the Hunstanton Sea Life Sanctuary. We particularly like the otter enclosure where you can see these playful water weasels fetch fish and frolic in the sun. www.sealsanctuary.co.uk

🔑 Slide down a sand dune. Gun Hill, near Burnham Overy Staithe, is a huge sand dune that's around sixteen metres high. The views from the top are fantastic, but it's even more fun to slide down to the bottom (on your bottom!).

Fascinating Facts

⭐ The Queen spends Christmas at Sandringham and summer at her house in Balmoral, in Scotland. Presumably she prefers the warmer winters down here in Norfolk!

⭐ The staff at Sandringham keep photos of all the cabinets in the palace. This means that when they remove their contents for dusting, they can put things back precisely where they were before.

When does a prince get wet? When he becomes the *raining* monarch!

PLAN YOUR VISIT 62

Sandringham House, Museum and Gardens

Sandringham Estate, Sandringham, PE35 6EB

www.sandringhamestate.co.uk

📞 01485 545408

🕐 Daily (Peak) 10.30-17.00

££ 🍴 🎁

I want to go here ☐

GO SEAL WATCHING

...at Blakeney Point

Although you can sometimes spot a seal in a zoo, we think it's far more fun to see them in their natural habitat. So this place definitely wins our *seal* of approval!

Blakeney Point is a strip of sand that stretches out into the sea. It's also a haven for seals – around 500 live in the area, and enjoy sunbathing on the sandbanks.

The Bean family have run boat trips from Morston to Blakeney Point for over 50 years. The boats go right up to the whiskered mammals, who are very friendly (and partial to the odd fish). You can even get out and picnic on the point!

Sticker Scores

5 ROYAL SEAL

4 SIGNATURE SEAL

3 WATERPROOF SEAL

2 WAX SEAL

1 RUBBER SEAL

Photo Op
Become a wildlife photographer and snap a sunbathing seal!

Make A Day Of It

 Go beachcombing at Wells-next-the-Sea. Look out for seashells, starfish, and maybe even a message in a bottle! www.wells-guide.co.uk

 Learn to paddleboard at Glide Surf School in Cromer. Paddleboarding is a bit like surfing, but you stand up and use an oar. This makes you less likely to fall off, which we think is pretty *oar*-some! www.glidesurfschool.co.uk

What do you call a seal that tells fibs?

Sea *lyin!*

Fascinating Facts

⭐ **There are 33 species of seal worldwide, but only two live in Britain. They are the grey seal and the common seal.**

⭐ People generally think of seals as swimmers, but they actually spend up to 90 per cent of their lives out of the water sunbathing on the sandbanks. It's just as well they don't suffer from sunburn!

⭐ **Seals can hold their breath underwater for up to one and a half hours.**

⭐ Seal is a musician from London who was famous in the 1990s. As far as we're aware he cannot hold his breath underwater for one and a half hours.

PLAN YOUR VISIT 63

Bean's boat trips
69 Morston Rd, Blakeney, NR25 7BD
www.beansboattrips.co.uk

📞 **01263 740505**

🕐 **Three or four departures a day, timetable dependent on tide.**

££

I want to go here ☐

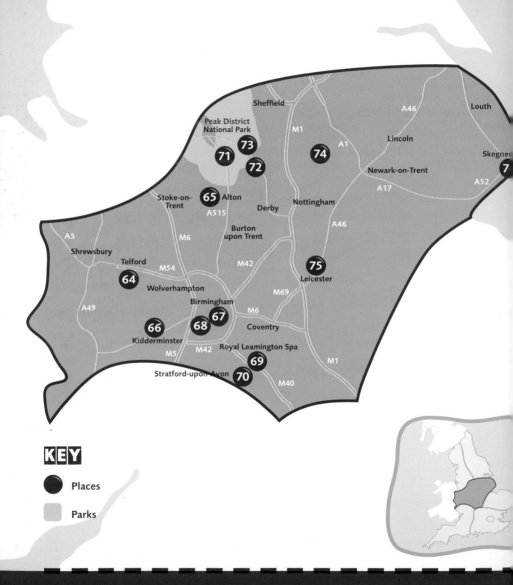

Sheffield

Peak District
National Park

A46   Louth

M1

Lincoln

71   **73**   **74**   A1   Skegness

72   A17   Newark-on-Trent   **7**

A52

Stoke-on-   **65** Alton   Nottingham   A46

Trent   A515   Derby

Burton
upon Trent

A5

Shrewsbury   M6

Telford   M42   **75**

M54   Leicester

64

Wolverhampton   M69

A49   Birmingham

66   **68** **67**   M6

Kidderminster   Coventry

M5   M42   Royal Leamington Spa

Stratford-upon-Avon   **69**   M1

70   M40

KEY

● Places

▇ Parks

LONDON

SOUTH EAST

SOUTH WEST

EAST

MIDLANDS

NORTH EAST

NORTH WEST

TOP FIVES

TRAVEL BACK IN TIME

...at Blists Hill Victorian Town

How do you turn the family car into a time machine? The answer's simple: use it to visit Blists Hill Victorian Town!

Blists Hill is a re-created Victorian town in the beautiful Ironbridge Gorge. It's one of ten museums celebrating the area's history as an industrial centre. Head to the Victorian Fairground for a go on a traditional carousel, then take a horse and carriage along Canal Street. You'll find a pharmacy containing a scary dentist's chair, and a sweet shop packed with tempting treats.

We suggest you finish your visit with a cone of traditional fish and chips from the fried fish seller. We *cod*'nt think of a *batter* way to end the day!

Sticker Scores

5 TIME MACHINE

4 EXCITING EXHIBIT

3 REGULAR RE-CREATION

2 MUNDANE MUSEUM

1 WASHING MACHINE

How do you transport herbs into the future?

With a *thyme* machine!

Make A Day Of It

🔑 Stand on the Iron Bridge. This famous structure was built in 1779 and was the world's first cast iron bridge.

🔑 Watch goats race at Hoo Farm Animal Kingdom near Telford. You can also see sheep competing in a steeplechase! www.hoofarm.com

Top Tip

Even the money used at Blists Hill is Victorian! Head to the town's bank to exchange your coins for shillings and pence.

Fascinating Facts

⭐ The expression 'to come a cropper' was used by the Victorians to mean losing your finger in a Cropper printing press. You can see one in the printer's shop at Blists Hill.

⭐ Queen Victoria may have been less than five foot tall, but she was made of tough stuff. She survived *seven* assassination attempts before dying of natural causes in 1901!

⭐ There's a good reason why Victorians look miserable in photos. In those days it took several minutes to take a single shot, and if you moved the picture would become blurry. Have a go at holding the same expression and you'll soon see why – it's much easier to maintain a miserable face than sustain a smile!

PLAN YOUR VISIT 64

Blists Hill Victorian Town
Coalport Road, Ironbridge, TF7 5DU
www.ironbridge.org.uk

📞 01952 433424

🕐 Daily (summer) 10.00-17.00
Daily (out of season) 10.00-16.00

£££

I want to go here ☐

MIDLANDS

HAVE A WHITE-KNUCKLE ADVENTURE

...at Alton Towers

The UK's largest theme park is built on the site of an historic stately home. But let's face it, you're unlikely to be coming here for a history lesson!

Alton Towers is a theme park and aquarium rolled into one. Forbidden Valley is the place to go for the seriously scary rides. Look out for Air, a 'flying' roller-coaster, then marvel at Ripsaw, which spins you around before soaking you with jets of water. It's like being in a giant washing machine (but without the dirty pants)!

We love the Flume in Katanga Canyon. You sit in a giant bathtub and zoom down the flume before being soaked by a huge power shower. If only bath-time was always this much fun!

Sticker Scores

5 ROLLER-COASTER

4 FANTASTIC FLUME

3 PASSABLE PIRATE SHIP

2 DOWNMARKET DODGEM

1 DRINKS COASTER

Top Tip
Some rides have height restrictions (especially in Forbidden Valley), so make sure you check the website for details before you visit.

Best Of The Rest

 Walk through a tunnel filled with sharks at Sharkbait Reef, the pirate-themed aquarium.

Make A Day Of It

 Brave the barefoot walk at Trentham Gardens in nearby Stoke-on-Trent. You'll tantalise your toes as you trek through mud, bark and babbling streams. And don't miss the Hide and Speak maze, which contains special pipes to help you talk your way out of trouble! www.trentham.co.uk/trentham-gardens

 Paint some pottery at Emma Bridgewater. Stoke-on-Trent is famous for ceramics (the area is known at The Potteries), so there's no better spot to paint a pot! www.emmabridgewater.co.uk

Fascinating Facts

★ The Ocean Tank Tunnel at Sharkbait Reef holds a million litres of water. That's enough to fill 25,000 bathtubs!

★ Thirteen (in Forbidden Valley) will travel about 47,000 miles during the current theme park season. That's the equivalent of two round trips to Australia (but without the in-flight movies)!

★ Oblivion is the fastest ride at Alton Towers, with a top speed of 75 miles per hour. That's faster than the UK motorway speed limit!

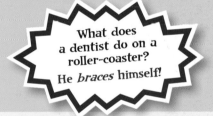

What does a dentist do on a roller-coaster? He *braces* himself!

PLAN YOUR VISIT 65

Alton Towers Resort
Alton, ST10 4DB
www.altontowers.com

📞 **0871 222 3330**

🕐 **Open daily from 10.00. Closing times vary – check website for details.**

£££

I want to go here ☐

LOUNGE WITH LEMURS

...at West Midland Safari Park

You might not think that the remote African island of Madagascar has much in common with the West Midlands. And largely you'd be right. But both *are* perfect places to look for a lemur!

The West Midland Safari Park has animals, rides and more besides. The highlight is the drive-through experience. This doesn't involve picking up a burger; it's a super safari which lets you get up close to cool cheetahs, rocking rhinos and awesome elephants. Look out for rare white lions – this place has more of them than any other zoo in the UK.

Sticker Scores

5 LOUNGING LEMUR	4 RECLINING RHINO	3 RELAXED RODENT
2 LAZY LIZARD	1 IDLE IGUANA	

Make sure you leave time to walk through Lemur Woods, in the African Village. There are three species of these Madagascan marvels, and daily feeding sessions take place during the summer.

Best Of The Rest

🔑 Feed the deer and goats from your car. You can buy a bag of special animal feed on arrival.

🔑 Take the Discovery Trail. You'll have some amazing animal adventures, from hanging with bats in the Twilight Cave, to peering at pythons in Mark O'Shea's Reptile World. Pick up a free scratch card quiz on your way into the park.

🔑 Ride the Rhino roller-coaster or get wet on the Zambezi Water Splash. Rides are paid for separately and height restrictions apply.

Fascinating Facts

⭐ **Lemurs are *scent*-sational animals. They have powerful smell glands which they use to communicate and mark out their territory. Males even compete for dominance by stink fighting, which involves covering their tails in stinky scent and wafting them at each other in a threatening manner!**

⭐ A lion's roar is the loudest of any big cat, and can be heard up to five miles away. We definitely wouldn't advise asking one to turn down the volume . . .

Top Tip
The lemur attraction is closed from November to March, so time your visit for the summer months if you want to see them.

PLAN YOUR VISIT 66

West Midland Safari and Leisure Park

Spring Grove, Bewdley, DY12 1LF

www.wmsp.co.uk

📞 **01299 402114**

🕐 **Opening times vary**

££

I want to go here ☐

WALK INSIDE A 17TH CENTURY PAINTING

...at Birmingham Museum and Art Gallery

Many galleries don't even let you touch the paintings, so it might come as a surprise to hear that this place lets you walk right inside one!

Birmingham Museum and Art Gallery houses over 40 galleries of cool collections. We love the interactive In Touch gallery, which lets you get touchy-feely with the exhibits.

The walk-inside painting is located next to the real version. It's three dimensional, so you can walk into it without doing any damage. We also love the talking heads – bronze busts of famous figures like Einstein which are positioned around a dinner table. Get up close and you'll even to get to listen in on the conversations! *Genius!*

Sticker Scores

5 — *ART* OF THIS WORLD

4 — PRECIOUS PICTURE

3 — AVERAGE ART

2 — DODGY DRAWING

1 — PITIFUL PAINTING

Top Tip

Look out for Big Brum – the clock tower that stands above the museum. It's Birmingham's version of Big Ben! Brum is a local name for Birmingham, and people from the city are known as Brummies.

Best Of The Rest

 See a deadly samurai sword in the In Touch gallery. You can also try on a replica Japanese mempo (face mask).

Make A Day Of It

 Be a crime-scene detective at Birmingham's superb science museum, Thinktank. www.thinktank.ac

 Hold a crab and touch a starfish in the interactive rock pools at the National Sea Life Centre in Birmingham. www.sealife.co.uk

Fascinating Facts

★ Kings and queens who posed for paintings often couldn't be bothered to sit around for long periods of time. Once their faces were finished, the artist would have to find other people to model for the arms, legs and feet.

★ Albert Einstein is one of the most famous scientists of all time, and people have tried to uncover the secrets behind his amazing intellect. His brain was removed from his body after death and then preserved by pickling so that it could be used for research.

Why did the painter collapse? He was having an *art* attack!

PLAN YOUR VISIT 67

Birmingham Museum and Art Gallery

Chamberlain Square, Birmingham, B3 3DH

www.bmag.org.uk

📞 0121 303 1966

🕐 Mon-Thu & Sat 10.00-17.00
Fri 10.30-17.00, Sun 12.30-17.00

FREE

I want to go here ☐

WANDER INTO A WORLD OF CHOCOLATE

... at Cadbury World

It's safe to say that there's no such thing as a world made of chocolate. But we reckon we've found the next best thing!

Cadbury World is a walk-through wonderland dedicated to everyone's favourite sweet treat. You can watch chocolatiers crafting confections in the chocolate making room, or have a go at creating your own in the Essence area. Just choose your ingredient (we love marshmallows) and watch as it's coated in liquid chocolate. *Mmmm!*

Sticker Scores

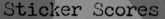

5	4	3
CHOCO-RIFFIC	*BAR*-RILLIANT	TREAT-TASTIC

2	1
MELT-DOWN	*CHOC* HORROR!

Don't miss Purple Planet, where you can chase chocolate eggs and even play in chocolatey rain! Stand in front of the camera then watch as your image is showered in chocolate buttons. Now that's one shower we wouldn't mind being caught in!

Best Of The Rest

🔑 Stock up on chocs at the Cadbury World Shop – it's the biggest Cadbury shop in the world!

Make A Day Of It

🔑 Go karting. Teamworks Karting offers instruction for over eights, so you'll be tearing around the track in no time. www.teamworkskarting.com

🔑 Meet a meat-eating plant in the subtropical house at The Birmingham Botanical Gardens. Look out for the pesky pitcher plant, which lures insects before drowning them in a pool of poison! www.birminghambotanicalgardens.org.uk

Photo Op
Take a picture of yourself surfing on a chocolate bar in front of the green screen (between the manufacturing zone and the packaging plant).

Fascinating Facts

★ Chocolate was first discovered by the ancient Aztec and Mayan peoples of Central America. They would grind up cacao (also known as cocoa) beans to make a spicy, dark drink.

★ According to legend, the Aztec ruler Emperor Montezuma drank 50 cups of hot chocolate a day. We assume he didn't bother with whipped cream and a flake . . .

★ It's official: chocolate really does makes you happy! The scientific reason is that it causes an increase in the levels of endorphins in the brain. Endorphins are a substance produced by the body, creating feelings of happiness.

PLAN YOUR VISIT 68

Cadbury World
Linden Road, Bournville, B30 2LU
www.cadburyworld.co.uk

📞 0844 880 7667

🕐 Opening times vary

£££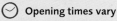

I want to go here ☐

TOUR THE TOWERS AND RAMPARTS

...at Warwick Castle

There was a time when a visit to Warwick Castle would probably have involved a bloody battle. Thankfully, these days you can tour its terrific towers without fear of being fired at!

Construction of Warwick Castle was begun by William the Conqueror in 1068. During the fourteenth century, two mighty structures were added – Caesar's Tower and Guys Tower. You can still climb them today, and the views from the top are *tower*-rific!

Don't miss the chance to ramble along the ramparts (the defensive walls of the castle). You can still look through the arrow slits that would have been used for firing at enemies – though thankfully these days you're unlikely to spot any attacking armies on the horizon!

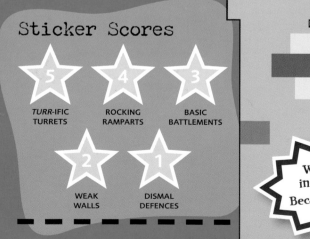

Sticker Scores

5 *TURR*-IFIC TURRETS

4 ROCKING RAMPARTS

3 BASIC BATTLEMENTS

2 WEAK WALLS

1 DISMAL DEFENCES

Why was it dark in medieval times?

Because there were so many *knights*!

Best Of The Rest

🔑 Check out the trebuchet. This medieval siege machine (used for attacking castles) fires a huge cannonball twice daily. It's an *explosive* sight!

🔑 Meet a dragon in The Dragon Tower. You'll be transported to Camelot, the legendary home of King Arthur, before coming face to face with a fire-breather!

Top Tip
Warwick Castle holds regular jousting displays. Check the website for an event schedule.

Fascinating Facts

⭐ It wasn't just cannonballs that were launched from trebuchets. Cows and manure were also fired to spread disease. The most popular animals were pigs, as they were thought to be the most aerodynamic and so would fly furthest.

⭐ Warwick Castle has a grisly murder hole in its gatehouse. This was used for dropping hot oil on top of enemy invaders!

⭐ In the Middle Ages, you could tell a man's rank by looking at his spurs (boot spikes used for steering horses). Lowly pages had tin spurs while higher ranking esquires would get silver ones. Gold spurs were reserved for knights and royalty.

PLAN YOUR VISIT 69

Warwick Castle
Warwick, CV34 4QU
www.warwick-castle.com

📞 0871 265 2000

🕐 Daily (summer) 10.00-18.00
Daily (out of season) 10.00-17.00

I want to go here ☐

STEP INTO SHAKESPEARE'S WORLD

...at Tudor World

England's most famous playwright did not just write dramatic plays and complicated tragedies, he also had an eye for witty one-liners. And one of his best-known comic characters was John Falstaff.

Tudor World re-creates the world of Falstaff as imagined by Shakespeare, in a building that the great man would have regularly visited. You can amble down a Tudor Street, accompanied by the authentic smells of life 500 years ago (imagine a mix of dung and rotting meat!). Brave the dingy dungeon or visit the barber surgeon as he performs a terrible tooth extraction! You can even watch Shakespeare writing his plays. That's one *Shakespeare*-ience you *Will* not want to miss!

(sign post)
ROMEO ◄
► JULIET ►
◄ HAMLET
BOTTOM ▼

Sticker Scores

5 PERFECT PLAYWRIGHT

4 ACCOMPLISHED AUTHOR

3 STANDARD SCRIBBLER

2 ROPEY WRITER

1 DIRE DRAMATIST

Top Tip

Catch a kids' production of one of Shakespeare's plays, performed by the Shakespeare 4 Kidz theatre company. Check www.shakespeare4kidz.com for the latest tour dates.

Best Of The Rest

🔑 Get put in the stocks during one of the Crime and Punishment shows that run during school holidays.

Make A Day Of It

🔑 Muck in at Mary Arden's Farm. This working Tudor farm has all kinds of rare breeds of animals, and you can also help out with traditional tasks like bread making.
www.shakespeare.org.uk

🔑 Ramble through a rainforest at the Stratford-upon-Avon Butterfly House. As well as colourful winged wonders, look out for the pet iguana. He can often be found resting on a heater to keep his tummy warm!
www.butterflyfarm.co.uk

Fascinating Facts

⭐ **William Shakespeare (also known as the Bard) was born in Stratford-upon-Avon in 1564. Most paintings show him as having facial hair, but no-one really knows if the Bard had a beard. After all, it's not like you can check his Facebook profile, and there are no surviving portraits from when he was alive.**

⭐ Shakespeare is believed to have written the world's first ever knock-knock joke. It appears in *Macbeth* (one of his most famous plays), but we won't quote it, as it's twenty lines long!

PLAN YOUR VISIT 70

The Falstaff Experience Tudor World

Sheep Street, Stratford-Upon-Avon, CV37 6EE
www.falstaffexperience.co.uk

📞 01789 298070

🕐 Daily 10.30-17.30

I want to go here ☐

GET ON YOUR BIKE

...on the Tissington Trail

It's not usually acceptable to tell someone to get on their bike. But in the Peak District, getting on your bike is a *wheel*-ly good thing!

The Tissington Trail runs along a disused train track between Asbourne and Parsley Hay, in the White Peak area of the Peak District National Park.

MY BIKE

These days, cyclists, horse riders and walkers are the only traffic you'll find here, so it's great for a family friendly ride. The full stretch is thirteen miles long, but shorter routes are available, and you can hire a bicycle from either end of the trail.

The views over the White Peak countryside are stunning, and there are pretty villages and picturesque picnic spots along the way. You'll have a *trail* of a time!

Sticker Scores

⭐ 5
BMX-CELLENT

⭐ 4
WHEEL-Y GOOD

⭐ 3
NI-CYCLE

⭐ 2
ON 'YER BIKE

⭐ 1
BMX-CRUCIATING

Make A Day Of It

🔑 Cross the stepping stones at Dovedale. These famous stones were built by the Victorians to help them cross the dramatic ravine. www.nationaltrust.org.uk

🔑 Creep through a cave at Poole's Cavern. This spooky limestone cave is filled with stalagmites and stalactites – weird rock formations that stick out from the floor and ceiling. www.poolescavern.co.uk

Similar Spots

🔑 The Monsal Trail is a traffic-free route that also runs along a disused railway line. www.peakdistrict.gov.uk

🔑 The Goyt Valley is one of the Peaks' most beautiful areas and is a great place to get on your bike. www.goytvalley.co.uk

Fascinating Facts

⭐ **The Peak District was Britain's first national park. Every year it receives between 17 and 21 million visitors! Thankfully they don't all choose to use the Tissington Trail at once . . .**

⭐ Believe it or not, the Peak District used to be a tropical lagoon! However, you can leave your snorkelling gear at home, because that was over 180 million years ago. Fossilised sea creatures and shells can still be spotted today in the limestone rocks and dry stone walls of the Peaks.

Top Tip
You can download a cycling guide and route maps from the website.

PLAN YOUR VISIT

The Tissington Trail
Parsley Hay to Ashbourne, Derbyshire
www.peakdistrict.gov.uk

FREE

I want to go here ☐

RIDE A CABLE CAR

...at the Heights of Abraham

The wild woodland park on **Masson Hill** has been attracting tourists for over two centuries. But before the cool cable car came along, getting there was nowhere near as ex-*hill*-erating!

The Heights of Abraham is a picturesque park with criss-crossing paths and trails.

There are also two prehistoric caverns that you can still tour today. The area was once an important centre for lead mining, but since then it has become a top tourist attraction.

To get to the top, you take the UK's first alpine-style cable car. It was built in 1984 and offers a thrilling journey that takes you as high as 65 metres above the Derwent Valley. So don't look down unless you have a head for heights!

Sticker Scores

5 RIDING HIGH

4 TREMENDOUS TRIP

3 JOLLY JOURNEY

2 ROTTEN RIDE

1 FLYING LOW

Top Tip
Your ticket includes a ride on the cable car, a guided cavern tour and access to the park. So leave plenty of time for your trip!

Best Of The Rest

🔑 Take an underground tour. We love the Great Masson tour, where special light effects flood the cavern with colour. Look out for calcite and fluorite crystals sparkling in blue, yellow and red.

🔑 Climb the Prospect Tower in the woodland park. It's a steep climb up the spiral staircase, but the views from the top are terrific.

Make A Day Of It

🔑 Ride the spiral slide in the awesome adventure playground at Chatsworth House.
www.chatsworth.org

Fascinating Facts

⭐ In Victorian times, tourists were lowered down to the caverns in baskets! At the bottom they were sold a candle to find their way around. However, the candles never lasted long, so visitors would usually have to fork out for another one to find their way back to the surface!

⭐ When you're touring Great Masson, look out for snotrock! This is the charming name given to the calcite deposits which trickle down the rock, resembling liquid bogeys. *Ewwww!*

Why did the toilet paper run down the hill? To get to the *bottom!*

PLAN YOUR VISIT 72

The Heights of Abraham
Upperwood Road, Matlock Bath, DE4 3PD
www.heightsofabraham.com

📞 01629 582365

🕐 Daily (peak) 10.00-16.30

£££

I want to go here ☐

GO ROCK SCRAMBLING

...with Aspire Adventure Activities

Rock scrambling has nothing to do with egg scrambling. It's actually an awesome outdoor challenge, and the Peaks are the perfect place to practice!

Rock scrambling involves activities such as climbing, weaseling and abseiling. It's a bit like an assault course, and is perfect for an open-air adventure. Aspire are based near Matlock in the Peak District. They run all day family rock scrambling activities at nearby Black Rocks. No experience is necessary, so don't worry if you're not a seasoned scrambler.

After your scramble, take a ramble! The rocks have been sculpted by wind and rain in to some spectacular shapes – see if you can spot the one that looks like a toad.

Sticker Scores

5 SCRAMBLED ROCKS

4 BOILED BOULDERS

3 SAUTÉED STONES

2 POACHED PEBBLES

1 GRILLED GRIT

What's a mountaineer's favourite music? *Rock 'n' Roll!*

Make A Day Of It

🔑 **Take a vintage tram ride** at Crich Tramway Village. www.tramway.co.uk

🔑 **Go canoeing** on Carsington Water – a reservoir south of Matlock. Carsington Sports and Leisure offer watersports activity days for kids during the school holidays. www.carsingtonwater.com

🔑 **Try on a cavalier's costume** and build your own castle in the Discovery Centre at beautiful Bolsover Castle. www.english-heritage.org.uk

Photo Op
Get a snap of you as you squeeze your way through a hole in the rocks. Just make sure you don't get stuck!

Fascinating Facts

⭐ **The world's biggest rock is Uluru (Ayer's Rock) in Australia. At 348 metres tall, it's around three and a half times the height of Big Ben!**

⭐ One of the strangest sports we've heard of is mountain unicycling. As the name suggests this involves pedalling over rough rocks on a unicycle. There are no brakes (though there might be some nasty *breaks* if you fall off!).

⭐ **The oldest rocks on Earth were found in northern Quebec in Canada. Geologists (people who study rocks and minerals) think they could be over four billion years old!**

PLAN YOUR VISIT 73

Aspire Adventure Activities
3 Unity Villas, Dale Road North, Darley Dale, DE4 2HX
www.aspireadventureactivities.co.uk

📞 **01629 732445**

🕐 **Tours (daily): 09.30 and 16.30 – book in advance**

£££

I want to go here ☐

SWING FROM TREE TO TREE

...in Sherwood Forest

If you like to monkey around, there's no better place to be king of the swingers than Go Ape!

Go Ape is a *tree*-mendous tree-top assault course high up in the heart of Sherwood Forest, in Nottinghamshire. The forest is the legendary home of Robin Hood and his band of merry men, so it's the perfect place for making some adventures of your own!

As long as you're over ten years old and 1.4 metres tall, you're all set for an un-*fir*-gettable forest experience. You'll need a head for heights as you clamber up ladders and hang onto Tarzan swings. There are even two tree-to-tree zip lines, which are believed to be the only ones of their kind In the UK. How *yew*-nique!

Sticker Scores

5 SHERWOOD FOREST

4 ROBIN HOOD

3 MERRY MEN

2 SHERIFF OF NOTTINGHAM

1 SHER-*WOOD*-N'T BOTHER

Top Tip

Every October, Nottingham Castle hosts a Robin Hood pageant. There's all kind of medieval merriment, from archery to falconry and jousting.

Make A Day Of It

🔑 Shoot a bow and arrow, Robin Hood style, at The Adrenalin Jungle. www.adrenalinjungle.com

🔑 See a world-famous tree. The 800 year old Major Oak is located in Sherwood Forest National Nature Reserve. According to legend, Robin Hood hid in its trunk to escape from the nasty Sheriff of Nottingham!

🔑 Witness a trial at the Galleries of Justice Museum. The museum is located in Nottingham's old courthouse and gaol. www.galleriesofjustice.org.uk

🔑 Get your skates on and take a beginners' lesson at The National Ice Centre in Nottingham. www.national-ice-centre.com

Fascinating Facts

⭐ **Robin Hood often appears in books and films wearing green tights and a tunic. Thankfully, this dodgy dress code does not apply at Go Ape!**

⭐ Go Ape has *branches* all across the UK. The highest Go Ape platform (at Grizedale Forest, in the Lake District) is eighteen metres above ground. That's taller than eleven gorillas standing on each other's heads (and almost as scary!).

How does Robin Hood tie his shoelaces? With a long bow!

PLAN YOUR VISIT 74

Go Ape! Sherwood Pines
Sherwood Pines Forest Park, Edwinstone, NG21 9JH
www.goape.co.uk

📞 **0845 094 8634**

🕐 **Open Feb-Nov (weekends only out of season). Opening hours vary**

£££

I want to go here ☐

SEE STARS

...at the National Space Centre, Leicester

Don't worry, we're not suggesting you get yourself a nasty knock on the head! At the National Space Centre there's a much safer way to see stars.

You can't miss the National Space Centre, as it's dominated by a 42 metre tower that houses three super-sized rockets. Inside, there are six galleries related to all things intergalactic, as well as a planetarium showing starry shows and planetary presentations.

We love the SIM (Spaceflight Induction Module) which you'll find in Tranquillity Base. Join the crew for a briefing, before climbing on board for a 3D mission to the ice moon, Europa. You'll brave meteor showers and radiation clouds before experiencing the hair-raising canyon run. It's *out of this world*!

Sticker Scores

5 SUPER-STAR	4 ASTONOMICAL	3 INTERGALACTIC

2 *MILKY WAY*-WARD	1 WASTE OF *SPACE*

Photo Op
Stand underneath the Thor Able rocket (in the Rocket Tower) and get someone to snap you as it blasts off!

Best Of The Rest

🔑 Take the astronaut challenge in Tranquillity Base and see if you have what it takes to travel through space!

🔑 Land a lunar module. Take the glass lift to the top of the Rocket Tower, where you'll get to pilot the Eagle lunar lander onto the surface of the moon.

Make A Day Of It

🔑 See snow leopards at Twycross Zoo. You can get a great view of these amazing animals from the re-created Himalayan Village. www.twycrosszoo.org

Fascinating Facts

⭐ Astronauts get taller in space! This is due to the absence of gravity pulling down on the spine.

⭐ Even outer space has had a fast-food delivery service! In 2001, Pizza Hut delivered a salami pizza to the International Space Station. We hope they didn't send the poor delivery man back for extra garlic bread!

⭐ One of the tallest mountains in our solar system is Olympus Mons on Mars. It's almost three times as tall as the Earth's highest peak, Mount Everest.

What do you do when you see a spaceman? You park in it, man!

PLAN YOUR VISIT 75

National Space Centre
Exploration Drive, Leicester, LE4 5NS

📞 www.spacecentre.co.uk

📞 0845 6052001

🕐 Tue-Fri 10.00-16.00
Sat-Sun 10.00-17.00
Open Mon-Sun during school holidays
– call ahead for details

£££

I want to go here ☐

GO BEACHCOMBING

...at Gibraltar Point Nature Reserve

Don't worry if you didn't pack your hairbrush! Beachcombing involves searching the shoreline for interesting items that have been washed up by the waves. So a bucket and spade will do fine.

Gibraltar Point Nature Reserve was set up to protect the plants and wildlife of this beautiful corner of the Lincolnshire coastline. The reserve stretches for three miles and includes areas of sand dunes, marsh and ponds.

Head to the beach to hunt for cool crabs, shiny shells and super starfish. Top of the spots is the Mermaid's Purse. This doesn't actually contain the mythical creature's pocket money – it's the egg case of a skate or ray. Whatever you find, you're *shore* to have fun hunting!

Sticker Scores

5 MERMAID'S PURSE

4 MINOTAUR'S MOBILE

3 UNICORN'S UMBRELLA

2 WITCH'S WALLET

1 DRAGON'S DOGGY BAG

Best Of The Rest

🔑 Go sea-dipping. The reserve holds regular events during the school holidays, including sea-dipping. You could find shrimps, flat fish and pipefish (a relation of the seahorse). Check the website for details.

🔑 Hide in a hide and spot birds. Watch out for the oystercatchers with their bright orange bills.

Make A Day Of It

🔑 Be beside the seaside in nearby Skegness. This seaside town has a pleasure pier with bowling, amusements and an indoor play area. There's also a brilliant beach for donkey rides and sandcastle building.

Fascinating Facts

⭐ **Gibraltar Point is like a big airport for birds (but without the passport control)! Large numbers of migrating birds pass through the point on their way to hotter countries.**

⭐ Starfish can grow new stomachs! When feeding, they push their tummies out through their mouths and into the shells of whatever they want to eat. If they are disturbed while feeding, they can bite off their stomach, crawl away and grow a new one. We definitely don't recommend you try this yourselves!

Top Tip
Check the tides before visiting – at high tide the road into Gibraltar Point can flood, leaving the Visitor Centre surrounded by water!

PLAN YOUR VISIT 76

Gibraltar Point National Nature Reserve

Gibraltar Road, Croft, Skegness, PE24 4SU

www.lincstrust.org.uk

📞 01754 898057

🕐 Daily (summer) 10.00-16.00
Mon-Fri (out of season) 11.00-15.00
Sat-Sun 11.00-16.00
Visitor Centre and café may be closed during bad weather

FREE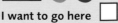

I want to go here ☐

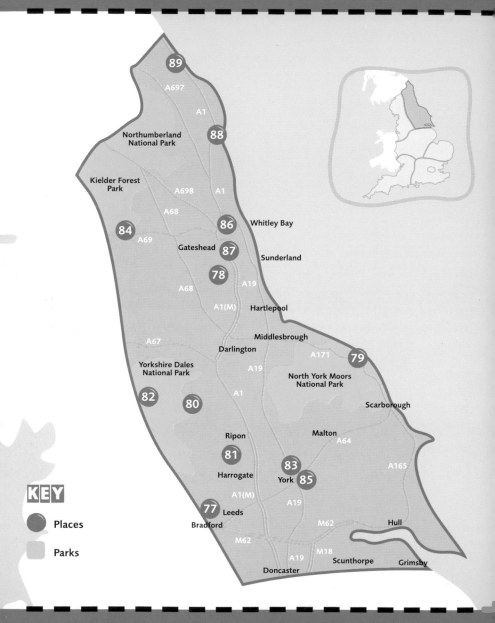

89

A697

A1

88

Northumberland
National Park

Kielder Forest
Park

A698

A1

A68

84

86

A69

Whitley Bay

Gateshead

87

Sunderland

78

A68

A19

A1(M)

Hartlepool

A67

Middlesbrough

Darlington

A171

79

Yorkshire Dales
National Park

A19

North York Moors
National Park

82

80

A1

Scarborough

Ripon

Malton

A64

81

Harrogate

83

York

85

A165

A1(M)

A19

77

Leeds

Bradford

M62

Hull

M62

A19

M18

Scunthorpe

Grimsby

Doncaster

KEY

● Places

▇ Parks

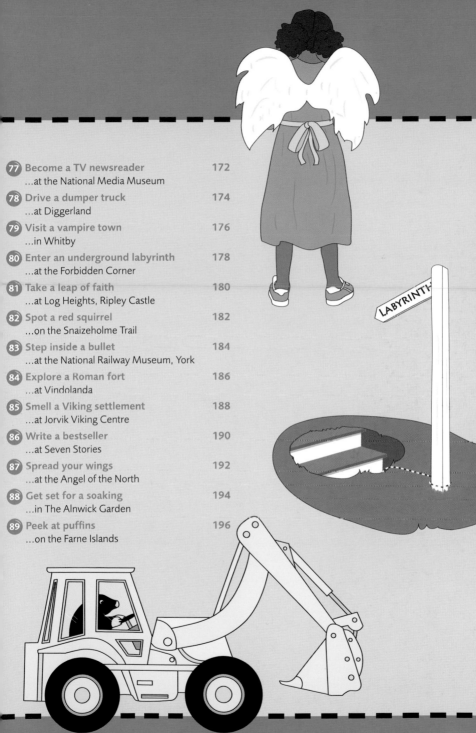

LONDON

SOUTH EAST

SOUTH WEST

EAST

MIDLANDS

NORTH EAST

NORTH WEST

TOP FIVES

LABYRINTH

BECOME A TV NEWSREADER

...at the National Media Museum

Have you ever watched a newsreader in action and thought 'I could do that'? **Well, at the National Media Museum you'll get to give it a go!**

The National Media Museum has eight floors of exhibits and galleries, all dedicated to the worlds of film, television and photography. There's also a giant IMAX screen showing the latest films in 3D.

We love the Experience TV gallery where you get to operate cameras for yourself in a replica studio. You'll find out how programmes are edited, and even have a chance to read the TV news.

Sticker Scores

5 BREAKING NEWS

4 HUGE HEADLINES

3 NEWSWORTHY NUGGET

2 AVERAGE ARTICLE

1 OLD NEWS

Wait for your prompt, then follow the day's events live on screen while listening to instructions from the director. Trust us, it's trickier than it looks!

Best Of The Rest

🔑 **Play vintage video games** in the Games Lounge. You'll get to have a crack at classics like Sonic the Hedgehog and Super Mario Kart.

Make A Day Of It

🔑 **Wield a weapon** at the Royal Armouries in Leeds. There are special handling sessions that let you get up close to wicked weapons and amazing armoury.
www.royalarmouries.org

🔑 **Go underground** at the National Coal Mining Museum in Wakefield. You'll get to don a hard hat and descend 140 metres for an unforgettable underground tour.
www.ncm.org.uk

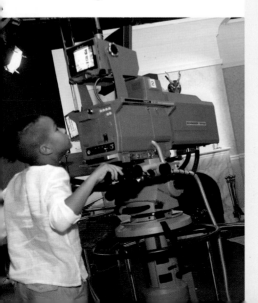

Fascinating Facts

⭐ **A British designer called Stuart Hughes has made the world's most expensive television set. It's worth £1.5 million, and is made using solid gold, diamonds and hand-sewn alligator skin. We think it's a rather *snappy* design!**

⭐ You might think that Hollywood is the world capital of film, but Bradford can also stake a claim to the title. It was designated the world's first city of film by UNESCO, the cultural part of the United Nations. The city has a fine film heritage dating back to World War One.

Photo Op
Get a snap of you standing in front of the blue screen in Experience TV. It'll look like you're at 10 Downing Street!

PLAN YOUR VISIT 77

The National Media Museum
Bradford, BD1 1NQ
www.nationalmediamuseum.org.uk

📞 **0844 856 3797**

🕐 **Tue-Sun 10.00-18.00**
Open Mondays during school and bank holidays

FREE

I want to go here ☐

DRIVE A DUMPER TRUCK

...at Diggerland

Have you ever wanted to drive a dumper truck? If so, we reckon you'll really *dig* this place!

Diggerland, near Durham, is a theme park devoted to diggers! Hop into the cab of a yellow JCB digger and take the controls. You can have a go at picking up ducks or knocking down skittles, or just dig a really big hole!

There are even mini Land Rovers that you can steer around specially designed courses.

Once you're done with digging, try one of the rides. On Spin Dizzy, you'll get to sit in the massive bucket of a digger's arm and fly through the air. Hold onto your hard hat!

Sticker Scores

5 TERRIFIC TRACTOR

4 DELIGHTFUL DIGGER

3 FINE FORK-LIFT

2 DODGY DUMPER TRUCK

1 PRO-*TRACTOR*

Make A Day Of It

 Steer down the Wear (the river that runs through Durham) on a rowing boat. Climb down the steps next to Elvet Bridge and hire a boat from Brown's Boathouse. Look out for a curious cow-shaped sculpture called the Durham Ox as you travel along.

 Feed the animals at Down at the Farm. Grab a bag of feed and you'll have deer and goats eating from the palm of your hand!
www.downatthefarm.co.uk

Top Tip

The vehicles have height restrictions, so check your height before you visit. However, you can still ride with a grown-up if you're not tall enough to drive alone.

Fascinating Facts

★ JCB have produced over 700,000 machines since 1954. That's enough to give one digger to every household in the North East!

★ The colour yellow is used a lot in the construction industry because it is so easy to see. So you'll see a whole lot of yellow at Diggerland.

★ *Yellow* is a famous song by the British band Coldplay. It includes the line 'It was all yellow', so we wonder if the band were at Diggerland when they wrote that one . . .

> What do you call a man with a spade on his head?
> *Dug*!

PLAN YOUR VISIT (78)

Diggerland Durham
Langley Park, County Durham, DH7 9TT
www.diggerland.com

 0871 227 7007

Opening hours vary

££

I want to go here ☐

VISIT A VAMPIRE TOWN

...in Whitby

Gather some garlic and wander down to Whitby, North Yorkshire's famous vampire town. Trust us, it's a *fang*-tastic day out!

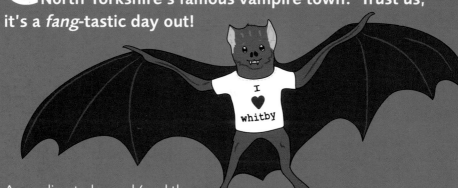

According to legend (and the famous novel by Bram Stoker), the vampire Count Dracula arrived in Whitby's port in the form of a huge black dog. He then scaled the 199 steps to St Mary's church on the cliff top and hid in the graveyard. You can re-trace his legendary steps and visit these spooky sites – just watch out for sinister-looking shapes skulking in the shadows!

Sticker Scores

5 FRIGHTFUL FANGS

4 A *BITE* OF ALRIGHT

3 *PARA*-NORMAL

2 BIG MI-*STAKE*

1 *FANGS* BUT NO THANKS!

If you're *thirsty* for more, don't miss Whitby's Dracula Experience, which has animation, special effects and 3D thrills. There's no place more spectacular to learn about Count Dracula!

> **How does Dracula like his coffee?**
> De-*coffin*-ated!

Best Of The Rest

🔑 Chomp on award-winning fish and chips at the Magpie Café. www.magpiecafe.co.uk

🔑 Fly a kite on West Cliff Beach in Whitby. This two mile sandy stretch is also perfect for sandcastle building.

Make A Day Of It

🔑 Get on your bike at Dalby Forest in the North York Moors National Park. There are 55 miles of mountain bike trails, as well as a brilliant bike park at Dixon's Hollow. www.forestry.gov.uk/dalbyforest

Fascinating Facts

⭐ **According to legend, garlic can be used to ward off vampires. So carry some with you if you're worried about vampire attacks while in Whitby!**

⭐ Local folklore says that Whitby was saved from a plague of serpents by St Hilda, who founded Whitby Abbey in 657 A.D. She supposedly threw the snakes off the cliffs then turned them into stone. This is the reason some people give for the snake-like spiral fossils in the rocks below Whitby's cliffs.

Top Tip

Look for a lucky duck! Whitby lucky ducks are world-famous good luck charms, which are handcrafted in glass. You can get them in shops all over the town.

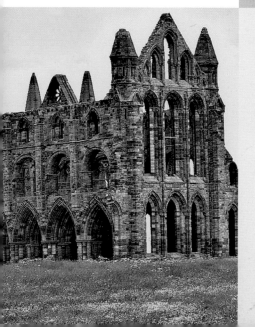

PLAN YOUR VISIT (79)

Dracula Experience
9 Marine Parade, Whitby, YO21 3PR
www.draculaexperience.co.uk

📞 **01947 601923**

🕐 **Daily (summer) 09.45-17.00**
Sat-Sun (out of season) 09.45-17.00

I want to go here ☐

NORTH EAST

ENTER AN UNDERGROUND LABYRINTH

...at the Forbidden Corner

Most corners are easy enough to get out of – you just turn round! But at the Forbidden Corner, nothing is quite as it seems . . .

The Forbidden Corner is a labyrinth of paths, tunnels and caves filled with all kinds of curiosities. You'll encounter giant statues, a glass pyramid, a talking horse, and even a waterfall you can walk right through!

The Temple of the Underworld is particularly perplexing. It's a bizarre underground maze with dark tunnels, whispering corridors, secret doors and illuminated fountains. There's no map, so it's up to you to find your way through!

Sticker Scores

5 MAGICAL MAZE

4 GLORIOUS GROTTO

3 DECENT DEN

2 TINY TUNNEL

1 LAME LABYRINTH

If you make it out, why not finish off with an ice-cream in the Herb Garden. We're sure you'll have a n-*ice thyme*!

Top Tip
Admission is by pre-booked ticket only, so make sure you reserve your place!

Best Of The Rest

Fawn over red deer in the Deer Park. The Forbidden Corner is set in the four-acre Tupgill Park, where you'll also find a fantastic fish temple.

Make A Day Of It

Try on medieval costume at Bolton Castle. You can also take a tour of the castle's secret passages and spiral staircases. www.boltoncastle.co.uk

See a golden eagle at the Bird of Prey Centre at Thorp Perrow Arboretum. There are daily flying demonstrations and a chance to meet and hold some of the birds. www.thorpperrow.com

Fascinating Facts

⭐ The Forbidden Corner was originally created as a private folly. Follies are buildings built as ornaments and decoration for gardens.

⭐ One of the world's most famous labyrinths is found in Greek mythology. It was built for King Minos of Crete and designed to hold the minotaur, a mythical creature that was half-man and half-bull. As far as we know, there aren't any minotaurs in the Forbidden Corner (or if there are, we haven't bumped into them yet!).

Photo Op
Find the Eye of the Needle and get a picture of you crawling through it. *Squeeeeze!*

PLAN YOUR VISIT 80

The Forbidden Corner
Tupgill Park Estate, Coverham, Leyburn, DL8 4TJ
www.theforbiddencorner.co.uk

📞 01969 640638

🕐 Mon-Sat (summer) 12.00-18.00
Sun (summer) 10.00-18.00
Open Sundays until December

££

I want to go here ☐

TAKE A LEAP OF FAITH

...at Log Heights, Ripley Castle

For reasons of sensible self-preservation, we wouldn't normally recommend plunging from a giant platform. But at Log Heights, it's all part of the fun!

Log Heights is a tree-top adventure in the grounds of Ripley Castle, near Harrogate. Experienced instructors will accompany you every step, leap and jump of the way, so it's a great place to *conker* your fears!

The Leap of Faith starts with a challenging climb to the top of a twelve-metre high platform. That's as tall as three double-decker buses! When you make it to the top, catch the trapeze bar (this bit is harder than it sounds!) and swing through the trees like Tarzan. Trust us, this daredevil jump will make your heart pump!

Sticker Scores

5 LEAP OF FAITH

4 JOYFUL JUMP

3 SATISFACTORY SKIP

2 LAZY LEAP

1 FELL OVER

Make A Day Of It

🔑 Try on armour on a guided tour of Ripley Castle. www.ripleycastle.co.uk

🔑 See a dancing bear. This is the name of one of the weird and wonderful rock formations on Brimham Moor. You might also spot a sphinx, find a flowerpot and get an cyeful of an eagle! www.nationaltrust.org.uk

🔑 Turn a hat to stone in the Petrifying Well at Mother Shipton's Cave. Weirdly, items placed in the well's waters eventually turn to stone due to the unusual minerals in the water. You'll see a stone Victorian top hat and a ladies bonnct left here in 1853! www.mothershiptonscave.com

Fascinating Facts

⭐ **A flea can jump as high as 100 times its body length. If this were the case for humans, we'd be able to leap over 45-storey buildings!**

⭐ The first ever bungee jumpers were the land divers of Pentecost Island in Vanuatu. These daring young men would jump from high wooden platforms with vines tied to their ankles to show off their courage and manliness.

What do you call a bear with no cars?

B!

PLAN YOUR VISIT 81

Log Heights
Ripley Castle, Harrogate, HG3 3AY
www.logheights.co.uk

📞 01423 711044

🕐 Sat-Sun & holidays 10.00-13.00; 14.00-17.00

£££

I want to go here ☐

SPOT A RED SQUIRREL

...on the Snaizeholme Trail

Red squirrels are native to England, but sadly they are now in danger of extinction. The Snaizeholme Trail leads to a red refuge, so it's the perfect place to marvel at these miniature mammals.

The Snaizeholme Trail is a picturesque ten-mile walk which leads to a viewing area in the Widdale red squirrel reserve – one of a number of protected areas set up to protect the reds. You can download written instructions and a map of the trail from the website.

Once you're at Widdale, look out for red squirrels playing and feeding in their beautiful woodland home. These tufty-eared creatures can be shy, so *squirrel* yourself away and keep your eyes peeled!

Sticker Scores

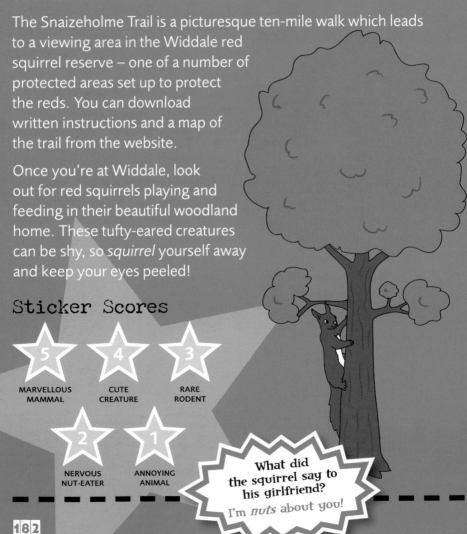

5 MARVELLOUS MAMMAL

4 CUTE CREATURE

3 RARE RODENT

2 NERVOUS NUT-EATER

1 ANNOYING ANIMAL

What did the squirrel say to his girlfriend?
I'm *nuts* about you!

Similar Spots

🔑 The forest around Thirlmere Reservoir in the Lake District is another refuge set up to protect reds. Rope bridges have even been installed to help them get safely from tree to tree! www.visitcumbria.com

🔑 Pensthorpe nature reserve in Norfolk has rare butterflies and kingfishers, as well as endangered red squirrels. You can also take a terrific tour in one of their camouflaged Land Rovers. www.pensthorpe.com

Make A Day Of It

🔑 Venture deep underground at White Scar Cave. You'll descend 150 metres below the surface and see prehistoric mud pools, ancient fossils and waterfalls rushing beneath your feet. www.whitescarcave.co.uk

Fascinating Facts

★ The red squirrel is native to the UK, but it is under threat from the American grey squirrel. Greys were first brought here over a hundred years ago. They are bigger and stronger, and they often take food that would otherwise be eaten by the reds. Greys also carry diseases which can be deadly to reds. So grey-free refuges like Snaizeholme help to protect reds from extinction.

Top Tip

The walk to the viewing area is a long one, so make sure you plan carefully and wear walking shoes.

PLAN YOUR VISIT 82

Snaizeholme Red Squirrel Trail
Widdale, Wensleydale
www.yorkshiredales.org.uk
 Open daily 24 hours
FREE

I want to go here ☐

STEP INSIDE A BULLET

...at the National Railway Museum, York

Don't worry, this bullet won't hurt you! We're talking about the Bullet Train, which is one of the speediest locomotives ever.

The National Railway Museum is the largest train museum in the world. It houses over 100 locomotives, including the world's fastest steam train (the *Mallard*) and the only Bullet Train to be found outside Japan. Bullets are terrific trains that can travel as fast as 275 mph. Step inside and imagine you were tearing down the tracks at top speed!

Don't miss the chance to have a nose around Queen Victoria's train. This 'palace on wheels' is so posh that there's even a bath on board! Whatever you *choo*-se to look at, we reckon you'll have a *rail* of a time!

Sticker Scores

⭐ 5 — FULL STEAM AHEAD

⭐ 4 — SPEEDING ALONG

⭐ 3 — ON THE RIGHT TRACK

⭐ 2 — OFF THE RAILS

⭐ 1 — ALL A-*BORED*

What's yellow and white and goes at 100 miles an hour?

A train driver's egg sandwich!

Make A Day Of It

🔑 Star in your own portrait at Beningbrough Hall – a beautiful old house with wonderful woods which are ideal for running around. Clever technology lets you insert your face into a well-known portrait, which you can then email to all your friends! www.nationaltrust.org.uk

🔑 Go glamping (glamorous camping) at Jollydays near York. There are no smelly sleeping bags here – just comfy beds and wood-burning stoves in every tent. There's even a communal tent where you can scoff tea and cake. www.jollydaysluxurycamping.co.uk

Fascinating Facts

★ For over 75 years a miniature railway (known as Mail Rail) operated beneath the streets of London, carrying letters from one side of the city to the other. It closed in 2003, but at its peak in the 1950s the railway delivered 12 million letters a day!

★ The longest station platform in England is at Colchester. At 620 metres it's as long as six football pitches laid end to end (though much less suitable for a kick-about)!

Photo Op
Sit in the driving seat of a locomotive in the Station Hall and pose as a train driver!

PLAN YOUR VISIT 83

National Railway Museum York
Leeman Road, York, YO26 4XJ
www.nrm.org.uk

📞 08448 153139

🕐 Daily 10.00-18.00

FREE

I want to go here ☐

EXPLORE A ROMAN FORT

...at Vindolanda

The Romans travelled all over Northumbria, but they weren't here to take a relaxing holiday. Instead they were building their awesome empire – at its peak it covered an area the size of Europe!

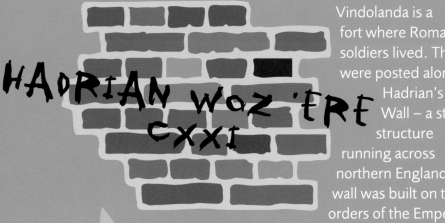

Vindolanda is a fort where Roman soldiers lived. They were posted along Hadrian's Wall – a stone structure running across northern England. The wall was built on the orders of the Emperor Hadrian and helped the Romans to protect their territory from invasion by the Scots.

Today you can explore the stone remains of the fort and even climb up a replica of Hadrian's Wall. And don't miss the bath house, where Roman soldiers enjoyed central heating in those chilly north-eastern winters!

Sticker Scores

5 WONDERFUL WALL

4 FABULOUS FENCE

3 PRACTICAL PARTITION

2 BOTCHED BORDER

1 UN-*FORT*-UNATE

How was the Roman Empire cut in half? With a pair of *Caesars*!

Make A Day Of It

🔑 Eat amazing ice cream at Wheelbirks Ice Cream Parlour, which is located on a working farm. Select your preferred flavours, then customise your cone with sauce and sprinkles. It's a chilly treat that's hard to beat! www.wheelbirks.co.uk

🔑 Go stargazing at Kielder Observatory. Book a Nightwatch and you'll get to learn the secrets of the sky, including how to find the Milky Way (the star-studded galaxy, not the chocolate bar!). www.kielderobservatory.org

Top Tip
You can still walk along the real remains of Hadrian's Wall today. The tallest parts are at Sycamore Gap. www.hadrians-wall.org

Fascinating Facts

⭐ In the 1970s, archaeologists unearthed the Vindolanda Tablets, which are the oldest surviving handwritten documents in Britain. Experts have pieced them together to get a fascinating insight into the life of a Roman soldier. For instance, letters have shown that soldiers at Vindolanda were so cold in winter that they wrote home asking for socks to wear with their sandals!

⭐ Romans liked their food. Although soldiers at a fort like Vindolanda would eat very basic rations, wealthier Romans would feast on delicacies like peacocks' tongues, stuffed dormice and even ostrich brains!

PLAN YOUR VISIT 84

Vindolanda Trust
Bardon Mill, Hexham, NE47 7JN
www.vindolanda.com

📞 01434 344277

🕐 Daily (peak) 10.00-18.00
Opening times vary out of season

££

I want to go here ☐

NORTH EAST

SMELL A VIKING SETTLEMENT

...at Jorvik Viking Centre

There are plenty of museums that show you things from the past. But at Jorvik you can smell the olden days too. It's ter-*whiff*-ic!

Jorvik Viking Centre (Jorvik is the Viking name for York) gives you a real sense for what life was like in Viking days. Your journey begins on board a state-of-the-art time capsule, which transports you along a Viking street. You'll get to peek into houses and backyards, and smell the authentic aromas. At one point you'll even see a man on the loo . . . you might want to hold your nose at this point!

Look out for the model Vikings who move and speak in their native language, Norse. Don't worry if you're not an expert on ancient languages; translations are provided!

Sticker Scores

5 *SCENT*-SATIONAL

4 PLEASING PERFUME

3 ACCEPTABLE AROMA

2 WOEFUL WHIFF

1 PUTRID PONG

Make A Day Of It

🗝 Face the torture chamber at York Dungeon. All being well you'll escape without a scratch! www.the-dungeons.co.uk/york

🗝 Gaze at gargoyles at York Minster, one of the largest cathedrals in Europe. Climb the 275 steps to the top and you'll be rewarded with an incredible view of the city and surrounding countryside. www.yorkminster.org

> **How did the Vikings send secret messages?**
>
> By *Norse* code

Fascinating Facts

⭐ **The Vikings used to wash their hair in urine to try and get rid of lice. *Wee*'ll stick with normal shampoo, thanks!**

⭐ One of the bloodiest figures in York's history is Eric Bloodaxe, who became the king of Jorvik in 940 A.D. As his name suggests, Eric was not someone to be messed with. He killed seven of his eight half-brothers when they tried to rebel against him!

⭐ **These days, York's city walls are a super spot for a scenic stroll. But hundreds of years ago, the four gates in the walls (called The Bars) were used for displaying the heads of criminals! The last head to linger there was that of the traitor James Mayne. His beheaded bonce was stuck on Micklegate Bar for nine years before finally being removed in 1754.**

PLAN YOUR VISIT 85

Jorvik Viking Centre

Coppergate, York, YO1 9WT

www.jorvik-viking-centre.co.uk

📞 01904 543400

🕐 Daily (summer) 10.00-17.00
Daily (out of season) 10.00-16.00

I want to go here ☐

WRITE A BESTSELLER

...at Seven Stories

Do you have what it takes to pen the next Potter? If so, Seven Stories could be the place to find your inspiration!

ONE
two
THREE
FOUR
FIVE
Six
SEVEN

Seven Stories is located in an old mill building, which happens to be seven *storeys* high! It's dedicated to the wonderful world of children's books and is home to loads of authors' manuscripts and original drawings. We love the regular events where you can meet famous authors and illustrators. They'll often be in the bookshop after the event signing copies of their books and sometimes even telling a story or two!

Before you leave, spend some time curled up with a good book on one of the purple leather sofas in the attic. It's a perfect way to end the day!

Sticker Scores

5 BRILLIANT BOOK

4 TERRIFIC TEXT

3 STANDARD STORY

2 DREADFUL DRAMA

1 NONSENSE NOVEL

What kind of stories do dogs like best? *Furry* tales!

Make A Day Of It

🔑 Look at life differently in the Life Science Centre. We love the hands-on Human Life exhibition where you can touch an Arctic ice wall, handle a heat sensitive camera and even build your own igloo! www.life.org.uk

🔑 Take the stadium tour at St James' Park, the home of Newcastle United. You can stand pitch-side, peer into the changing rooms and admire the view from the stadium. www.nufc.co.uk

Top Tip
Author events usually have a small booking fee, so call ahead for details and to secure your place.

Fascinating Facts

⭐ The most expensive manuscript ever sold was Leonardo Da Vinci's Codex Leicester, which fetched almost £20 million at auction in 1994. That's enough to buy two million copies of *England Unlocked*!

⭐ *The Bible* is the most translated book of all time. It's available in around 438 different languages, including Klingon – the alien language used in the science fiction series *Star Trek*!

Photo Op
There are loads of costumes to try on in the attic. Strike a pose dressed up as a character from your favourite story.

PLAN YOUR VISIT 86

Seven Stories
Lime Street, Ouseburn Valley,
Newcastle-upon Tyne, NE1 2PQ
www.sevenstories.org.uk

📞 0845 271 0777

🕐 Mon-Sat 10.00-17.00
Sun & bank holidays 10.00-16.00

££

I want to go here ☐

SPREAD YOUR WINGS

...at the Angel of the North

Angels are supposed to live in the heavens, but this one has somehow ended up in Gateshead. We like to think its wide-open wings send a message of welcome to the North East.

The Angel of the North is a stunning steel structure with wings that are as wide as those on a jumbo jet! It was designed by a famous sculptor called Anthony Gormley and can withstand winds of over 100 miles per hour.

You can see the Angel from a long way away, but it's also fun to visit. Why not tickle its toes or wonder at its wings from below? It's a *heavenly* day out!

Sticker Scores

5 AWESOME ANGEL

4 WONDERFUL WINGS

3 SHINING HALO

2 SAD STATUE

1 SCRAP METAL

Make A Day Of It

🔑 Cross the Tyne on the Gateshead Millennium Bridge. This superb structure is the world's first tilting bridge. It looks like a winking eye as it opens and shuts to let ships through. www.gateshead.gov.uk

🔑 Make your own music at The Sage (the building that looks like a giant caterpillar on the side of the river Tyne). It holds regular workshops for families and schools, so you can try your hand at samba drumming or singing with a choir. www.thesagegateshead.org

How do Angels greet each other?
Halo!

Fascinating Facts

⭐ The Angel is over 20 metres tall – that's higher than four double-decker buses (though less useful if you need to pop to the shops!).

⭐ In 1998 fans of Newcastle United football team used a combination of fishing line, rubber balls and catapults to put a huge replica of striker Alan Shearer's famous shirt over the Angel! It stayed on for 20 minutes, before police arrived at the scene and took it off.

Photo Op
Stand away from the Angel with your arms outstretched. Get someone to crouch down and take a picture with the Angel in the background. If they get the angle right you'll look as tall as the sculpture!

PLAN YOUR VISIT 87

The Angel of the North
Durham Road, Low Eighton, Gateshead, NE9 6AA
www.gateshead.gov.uk
📞 0191 478 4222
FREE

I want to go here ☐

GET SET FOR A SOAKING

...in The Alnwick Garden

Have you ever been sprayed by a sprinkler in your garden? Well, times that by 100 and you're halfway to imagining what it feels like to get caught in the giant jets of The Alnwick Garden's Grand Cascade!

The garden is located close to the town's cool castle, which was Hogwarts (from the outside) in the Harry Potter movies. It's a fabulous place, complete with a giant tree house, wobbly bridge and treetop walkway. There's even a poison garden, where guides will tell you stories of poisonous plants and fearsome flowers!

We love dodging the jets in the Grand Cascade. Just remember to bring a spare set of clothes. However quick you are, we're willing to bet that you're going to get wet!

Sticker Scores

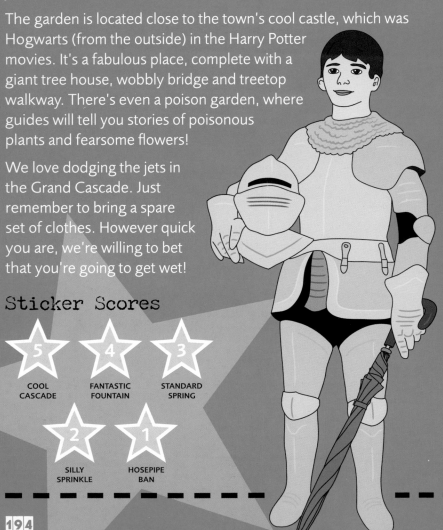

5 COOL CASCADE

4 FANTASTIC FOUNTAIN

3 STANDARD SPRING

2 SILLY SPRINKLE

1 HOSEPIPE BAN

Make A Day Of It

🔑 Enter a medieval world at Alnwick Castle. Dress up as a knight in Knight's Quest, or come face to face with ghosts, ghouls and a mythical creature in Dragon Quest. www.alnwickcastle.com

🔑 Spot the wild white cattle in the grounds of Chillingham Castle. You may not have herd about the white cattle of Chillingham, but they're thought to be the only wild cattle in the world. www.chillingham-castle.com

How do you dance in the bath?
Using *tap* water!

Fascinating Facts

⭐ These days, eleven year olds are too busy with their school work to think about going into battle. But Sir Harry Hotspur, who lived in Alnwick Castle, had already been knighted for bravery by the time he reached his twelfth birthday.

⭐ The tree house at The Alnwick Garden is the largest in the world. It has toilets and a 120 seat restaurant!

Top Tip
Buy a combined ticket for the castle and the garden – it's cheaper than getting two separate ones.

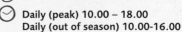

PLAN YOUR VISIT 88

The Alnwick Garden
Denwick Lane, Alnwick, NE66 1YU
www.alnwickgarden.com

📞 01665 511350

🕐 Daily (peak) 10.00 – 18.00
Daily (out of season) 10.00-16.00

££

I want to go here ☐

PEEK AT PUFFINS

...on the Farne Islands

Nothing quite compares to a puffin! And there's no better place to spy these black-and-white seabirds than the Farne Islands. 100,000 pairs of them gather on the rocks there each year.

The Farnes are a group of islands off the Northumberland coast. People come here to gawp at grey seals, peer at puffins and see seabirds. The best time to come is in the nesting season, between May and July. Boat trips leave from Seahouses and a round trip takes about three hours.

Watch out for the arctic terns, who are famous for dive bombing towards unsuspecting visitors. We suggest you *tern* away if you see one heading in your direction!

Sticker Scores

⭐ 5	⭐ 4	⭐ 3
PUFFIN	DUCK	GANNET

⭐ 2	⭐ 1
PIGEON	*NUFFIN'*

Make A Day Of It

🔑 **Chomp on fish and chips** in Seahouses when your boat trip returns.

🔑 **Bound around Bamburgh Castle.** This fine Norman fortress sits dramatically atop a rocky outcrop, overlooking the Farne Islands. The beach below is great for sandcastle-building. www.bamburghcastle.co.uk

🔑 **Cross the causeway** to Lindisfarne. This raised road connects the island to the Northumberland mainland and disappears under the sea at high tide. So make sure you check the tide times before you travel! When you get there, look out for grey seals resting on the rocks at Sandham Bay.

Fascinating Facts

⭐ **Puffins are sometimes called the 'clowns of the sea'. But think twice before booking one for your birthday bash. The name refers to their brightly coloured beaks and exaggerated way of walking rather than their circus skills!**

⭐ Grace Darling was the daughter of a lighthouse keeper on the Farne Islands. In 1838, aged just 22, she rescued nine people from a shipwreck with her dad, using just a rowing boat. That's one Amazing Grace!

Why was the bird out of breath?
Because he was *puffin*!

PLAN YOUR VISIT 89

Farne Islands

Off the Northumberland coast
www.nationaltrust.co.uk

🕐 Boat trips daily (summer): hourly from 10.00-16.30 Several companies sail from Seahouses harbour Out of season trips by arrangement

££

I want to go here ☐

NORTH WEST

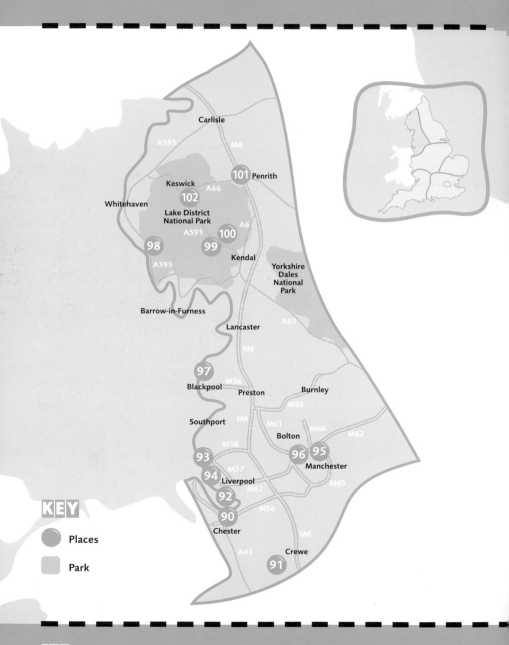

Carlisle

A595

M6

101 Penrith

Keswick
102
A66

Whitehaven

Lake District
National Park
A591
100

98
99

A595

Kendal

A6

Yorkshire
Dales
National
Park

Barrow-in-Furness

Lancaster

A65

M6

97

Blackpool
M56
Preston
Burnley

M65

Southport
M6
M61

M66
M62

Bolton
M58

96 95

93
M57
Manchester

94
Liverpool
M62
M60

92
M56

90
M6

Chester

A41
Crewe

91

KEY

● Places

▇ Park

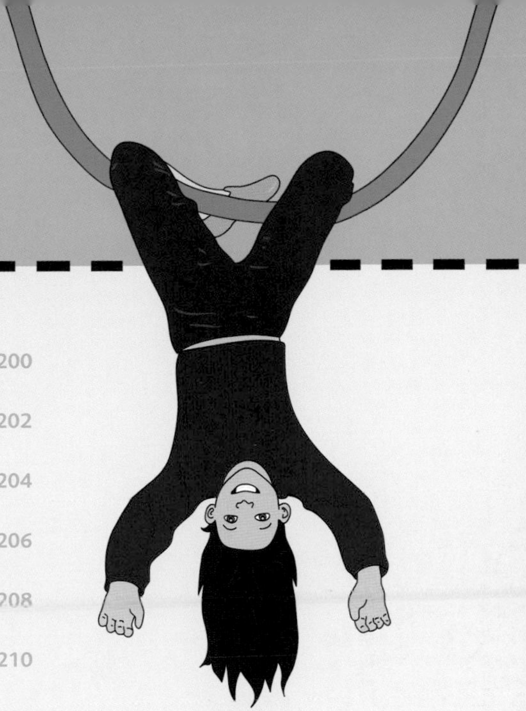

LONDON

SOUTH EAST

SOUTH WEST

EAST

MIDLANDS

NORTH EAST

NORTH WEST

TOP FIVES

HANG WITH AN ORANG-UTAN

...at Chester Zoo

Chester isn't exactly an obvious place to spot an orang-utan. But at the city's zoo you can roam around a re-created rainforest that's home to thirteen of these awesome apes!

Chester Zoo is an award-winning animal attraction where you'll find around 7,000 animals. The zoo is also involved in helping with the conservation of endangered species, including orang-utans.

The Realm of the Red Ape has both Sumatran and Bornean orang-utans. As you wander along the walkway, watch out for the touch pads that teach you all about their natural habitat. And keep your eyes peeled for the Realm's reticulated pythons. At up to ten metres long, these slippery characters are the longest snakes in the world!

Sticker Scores

5 OUTSTANDING ORANG-UTAN

4 AMAZING APE

3 CHEEKY CHIMP

2 GRUFF GORILLA

1 CHEEKY MONKEY

Best Of The Rest

🔑 Get up close to Komodo dragons in the Islands in Danger exhibit. These large lizards are believed to be the most intelligent reptiles in the world. Sadly they aren't much use in helping you with your homework!

Make A Day Of It

🔑 Ramble with a Roman on a Chester Roman tour. A costumed centurion will be your guide on an entertaining trip through the city's Roman history. www.romantoursuk.com

🔑 Float down the river on a leisurely Chester Boat river cruise. You can combine your ticket with an open top bus ride through the city. www.chesterboat.co.uk

Fascinating Facts

⭐ **Chester Zoo's animals eat a combined 400 tonnes of fruit and vegetables daily. So it's safe to say they're getting their five a day!**

⭐ Depending on the size of each meal, adult pythons may only need to eat two or three times a year. But don't be worried about them wasting away. They can dislocate their jaws when feeding, allowing them to gorge on a whole animal in one go!

Photo Op
Strike a pose with an orang-utan (well, a life-sized photo of one, anyway) in the Realm of the Red Ape.

PLAN YOUR VISIT 90

Chester Zoo
Upton, Chester, CH2 1LH
01244 380280

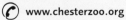 www.chesterzoo.org

🕐 **Opens daily at 10.00. Closing times vary.**

£££

I want to go here ☐

TAKE A SPY TRAIL

...at Hack Green Secret Nuclear Bunker

At Hack Green you can experience all the excitement of being a secret agent without having to change your name and identity!

Hack Green is a mysterious place located deep in the Cheshire countryside. During the Cold War it was set aside as a top secret government headquarters. In the event of a nuclear attack, the bunker would have sheltered government officials while they worked to rebuild the country.

Pick up a Mouse Trail sheet on your way in to the bunker. Your mission is to identify as many mice as you can. You'll find them hiding in Hack Green's spooky rooms and corridors. But beware – this is a very big place and these treacherous rodents could be anywhere. Can you *hack* it?

Sticker Scores

5 MISSION ACCOMPLISHED

4 AGENT APE

3 COVERT COBRA

2 SECRETIVE SWAN

1 MISSION IMPOSSIBLE

Best Of The Rest

🔑 See a real nuclear bomb in the Hack Green Museum. Thankfully the exploding bits have been taken out!

Make A Day Of It

🔑 Take the Crocky Trail. This mile-long adventure trail has mazes, swings, bridges and tunnels. Be prepared to get very muddy!
www.crockytrail.co.uk

🔑 Look out over eight counties at Beeston Castle. The ruins of this medieval marvel sit on top of a rocky crag. On a clear day you can see from the Pennine Hills to the Welsh Mountains.
www.english-heritage.org.uk

🔑 Eat amazing ice-cream at Cheshire Ice Cream. You're allowed a free sample to help you choose, so make sure you try before you buy!
www.cheshirefarmicecream.co.uk

Fascinating Facts

★ **The Cold War was a tense conflict between the USA and the UK on one side and Russia on the other. It lasted from around 1946 to 1991. While there was never any direct fighting, many people feared a devastating descent into nuclear war.**

★ The British government was so worried about the Cold War that they produced an information film to show on all television stations three minutes before a nuclear attack. You can see it at Hack Green.

What do secret agents eat at Christmas?
Mince *spies!*

PLAN YOUR VISIT 91

Hack Green Nuclear Bunker
Nantwich, CW5 8BL
www.hackgreen.co.uk

📞 Daily (summer) 10.30-17.30

🕐 Fri-Sun (out of season) 11.30-16.30 (closed in December)

££

I want to go here ☐

SWIM WITH SHARKS

...at Blue Planet Aquarium

Don't worry, we're not suggesting you swim with a man-eating monster! At Blue Planet Aquarium you can take an unforgettable dip in shark-infested water without risking your life.

Blue Planet Aquarium is home to Europe's largest selection of sharks. The Junior Shark Dive experience lets you swim with all kinds of colourful fish – including a selection of finned friends. Look out for zebra sharks, black and white tip sharks and the curiously named wobbegong.

If you don't fancy taking the plunge, you can still spot aquatic creatures as you walk through the aquarium's glass covered Aquatunnel. And don't miss the chance to touch starfish and rays at Where the Land Meets the Sea. You'll have a *ray*-lly good time!

Sticker Scores

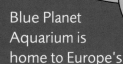

5 JAWS

4 SHOCKING SHARK

3 REMARKABLE RAY

2 PITIFUL PLANKTON

1 SNORES

What do you call a fish with no eyes?

Fsh!

Best Of The Rest

🔑 Come face to face with a tarantula in Venom. Specially reinforced displays let you get up close to a whole host of venomy enemies, from scorpions to stinging jellyfish.

🔑 Learn about life underwater in one of the Aquatheatre shows.

Make A Day Of It

🔑 Shop 'til you drop. Around the corner from Blue Planet is Cheshire Oaks - a huge designer village with lots of shops and restaurants. There's also a sixteen-screen cinema and bowling alley.

🔑 Journey through space in Spaceport's 360-degree Space Dome. This ace space place has six galleries full of interactive exhibits. www.spaceport.org.uk

Fascinating Facts

⭐ **The Aquatunnel at Blue Planet can withstand the weight of three elephants. That's reassuring when there's only a sheet of glass separating you from a selection of sharks!**

⭐ Sharks can sense a single drop of blood among a million drops of water. They can also hear a fish approaching from over a mile away.

Top Tip

You need to be at least eight years old (and confident in the water) to do the shark swim. Check the website for details and make sure you book in advance.

PLAN YOUR VISIT 92

Blue Planet Aquarium
Longlooms Road, Cheshire Oaks, Ellesmere Port, CH65 9LF

www.blueplanetaquarium.co.uk

📞 **0151 357 8804**

🕐 **Opens daily at 10.00 – closing times vary.**

£££

I want to go here ☐

CREATE YOUR OWN ART

...at Tate Liverpool

You might think galleries are all about peering at paintings. But at Tate Liverpool you can actually have a go at making your own masterpiece!

Tate Liverpool is located in the city's Albert Dock and is home to the largest collection of modern art in the North of England. The family room is open all year round and has craft, drawing and art materials available. So we think it's great to create at the Tate!

Alternatively, ask at the foyer for the free Little Long Large sketchbook. It contains loads of interactive activities that will keep you entertained while you're admiring art and staring at sculpture.

Sticker Scores

5 MASTERPIECE

4 CRACKING CANVAS

3 SATISFYING SKETCH

2 DISAP-*PAINTING*

1 DISASTER-*PIECE*

Why did the painting go to jail?
Because he had been *framed!*

Best Of The Rest

Stare at ships from the windows of the dockside galleries. You'll see the Mersey ferries – and possibly even a passing duck (see p208)!

Make A Day Of It

Amble round Albert Dock. In its prime, this historic dock was filled with ships carrying valuable cargoes from across the world. The dock closed in 1972, but it has since been renovated and is now home to museums, shops and restaurants, as well as Tate Liverpool.
www.albertdock.com

Tour the turf at Anfield, the home of Liverpool Football Club. You'll get to walk through the players' tunnel and touch the famous 'This is Anfield' sign. www.liverpoolfc.tv

Fascinating Facts

★ The most expensive painting ever sold at auction was by American artist Jackson Pollock. It went under the hammer in 2006 for an *art*-rageously expensive £70 million pounds!

★ The smallest sculptures in the world are so tiny they can only be seen through a microscope! These mini-marvels, by British sculptor Willard Wigan, include a model of an astronaut and the Incredible Hulk!

Photo Op
Position yourself carefully behind the basketballs in Jeff Koons' *Three Ball Total Equilibrium* and it'll look as though you have a basketball for a head!

PLAN YOUR VISIT 93

Tate Liverpool
Albert Dock, Liverpool, L3 4BB
www.tate.org.uk/liverpool

📞 0151 702 7400

🕐 Daily 10.00-17.00

FREE

I want to go here ☐

RIDE A DUCK

...on The Yellow Duckmarine

Buses, taxis and cars are the obvious choices for getting around a city. But in Liverpool, you can tour the docks on a duck!

OK, the Yellow Duckmarine may not have feathers or eat crusts of stale bread. It's actually a DUKW – an amphibious vehicle that can move on both land and water. DUKWs were really useful during World War Two, as they reduced the time it took to load stuff on and off ships.

The tour starts on dry land and takes in some of Liverpool's superb sights, including its two famous cathedrals. You'll then splash into the South Docks for a wonderful waterborne tour. Trust us, it's never been so cool to ride around the 'pool!

Sticker Scores

5 — DUCK TOUR

4 — GOLDEN GOOSE

3 — SIMPLE SWAN

2 — *BEAK MISTAKE*

1 — *DUCK BORE*

Similar Spots

🔑 Why not take a traditional trip on a world-famous Mersey ferry? They run from Albert Dock to Seacombe and Birkenhead on the Wirral. www.merseyferries.co.uk

Make A Day Of It

🔑 See inside a World War Two submarine at U-Boat Story. You can get there from Liverpool on the Mersey ferry. www.u-boatstory.co.uk

🔑 Drive through a baboon jungle at Knowsley Safari Park. You'll also get to look at lions, gaze at giraffes and chill with camels in this super safari park. www.knowsleysafariexperience.co.uk

🔑 Watch glass being made at World of Glass. Head to the studio where you'll get to see boiling-hot glass being moulded using traditional tools. www.worldofglass.com

Fascinating Facts

⭐ **Liverpool is the place to see rubber duckies race! Every year, the city holds a charity event in which up to 40,000 rubber ducks float along a stretch of the Liverpool-to-Leeds canal. You'd need a pretty big bathtub to re-create that at home!**

⭐ The name Yellow Duckmarine comes from the song *Yellow Submarine* by Liverpool's most famous band, The Beatles. Liverpool is very proud of The Fab Four (as they were known), and there's even a museum dedicated to them in Albert Dock.

What time do ducks wake up? At the *quack* of dawn!

PLAN YOUR VISIT 94

The Yellow Duckmarine
Anchor Courtyard, Albert Dock, Liverpool, L3 4AS
www.theyellowduckmarine.co.uk

📞 0151 708 7799

🕐 Daily tours from 10.30

££

I want to go here ☐

...at the Museum of Science and Industry

Babies are cute, but you probably wouldn't trust one to perform complex calculations. So it may come as surprise to hear that the world's first computer was named the Baby!

The Museum of Science and Industry contains awesome exhibits and activities linked to Manchester's industrial heritage. Amongst them is a replica of the Baby – a pioneering number-crunching machine built in 1948 by the city's university. Be prepared to see something a tad bigger than an iPad – it has roughly the same proportions as a small bedroom!

In other parts of the museum you can crawl through a smelly, re-created Victorian sewer! Keep an eye out for rats and poo as you weave your way through . . .

Sticker Scores

5 MAGNIFICENT MACHINE

4 COOL COMPUTER

3 PASSABLE PC

2 DODGY DEVICE

1 HOPELESS HARD DRIVE

Best Of The Rest

🔑 Stare into an infinity mirror in the experiment gallery. You'll see yourself in lights, and multiplied to infinity in all directions!

🔑 Meet a dinosaur at The Manchester Museum. They've got a cast of a terrifying T. rex skeleton. Check out the teeth – they're the size of big bananas!
www.museum.manchester.ac.uk

🔑 Try on a trendy trilby or a brilliant bowler in the dressing-up room at Hat Works in Stockport. It's the UK's only museum dedicated to headwear. www.hatworks.org.uk

Why did the computer get glasses?
To improve its web-*sight*!

Fascinating Facts

★ **The Baby's proper name is The Manchester Small-Scale Experimental Machine. No wonder they shortened it to something simpler!**

★ Manchester's population grew rapidly in the late 1800s, creating huge amounts of sewage. So in 1877 the Holt Town Works were set up to turn human waste into concentrated manure. It was so popular that it was sold as far afield as Jamaica!

Top Tip
Look out for Manchester's trams! These super streetcars crisscross the city, carrying a *tram*-azing 20 million passengers every year! Deansgate station is a five minute walk from the museum.

PLAN YOUR VISIT 95

MOSI (Museum of Science & Industry)
Liverpool Road, Castlefield, Manchester, M3 4FP
www.mosi.org.uk
📞 0161 832 2244
🕐 Daily 10.00-17.00
FREE

I want to go here ☐

SHOP UP A STORM

...at the Trafford Centre

All shopping centres have shops, obviously. Some also have a few restaurants. But the Trafford Centre is the only one we know that's also home to an enormous indoor ski slope!

The Trafford Centre is a shopping centre, restaurant world and leisure village all rolled into one. So after you've been window shopping in the dazzling designer boutiques you can practice your putting at Trafford Golf Centre, or feel what it's like to fly in the indoor skydiving centre.

Sticker Scores

5 CLASSY CLOTHES

4 COOL COMPUTERS

3 SUPER STALLS

2 PRICEY PANTS

1 SHOPPED OUT

However, the highlight has to be the Chill Factore winter sports centre. Weave your way down the indoor ski slope or zoom along the 60 metre luge slide. It's not just cold; it's *brrr*-illiant!

Best Of The Rest

🔑 Mooch round a mini Manchester at Legoland Discovery centre, which is also in the Trafford Centre. www.traffordcentre.co.uk

Make A Day Of It

🔑 Take the Old Trafford stadium tour. Explore Manchester United's club museum, then pop into the Red Café. Keep your eyes peeled for United players – apparently they like to lunch here! www.manutd.com

🔑 Peer at deer in Tatton Park. As well as the 1,000 acre deer park, there are also beautiful gardens, a maze, an adventure playground and a farm with rare animal breeds. www.tattonpark.org.uk

Fascinating Facts

⭐ **The Trafford Centre is housed in four buildings over 140,000 square meters of space. That's about the size of seventeen football pitches!**

⭐ Chill Factore's snow is made overnight by chilling the whole place to minus six degrees Celsius. Water cannons are then used to create clouds of vapourised water which then freezes to become snow. We think being Chief Snow Creator at Chill Factore must be the *coolest* job ever!

> **Customer:**
> Can I try on that dress in the window?
> **Shopkeeper:**
> No, you'll have to use the changing room like everyone else!

PLAN YOUR VISIT 96

The Trafford Centre
Manchester, M17 8AA
www.traffordcentre.co.uk

📞 0161 749 1717

🕐 Mon-Fri 10.00-22.00
Sat 09.00-21.00
Sun 12.00-18.00

FREE* - £££

*It depends on what you choose to do!

I want to go here ☐

LOOK THROUGH THE EYE OF A TOWER

...at Blackpool Tower

Blackpool Tower may not have actual eyes, but this skyscraper by the sea does have a del-*eye*-tful observation deck!

Blackpool Tower is located on the Promenade (the road that runs along the seafront). At 158 metres tall, it's pretty hard to miss!

You can head to the top as part of the Tower Eye experience. This starts with a 4D cinema show, complete with wind, rain and smoke. You then take the lift to the top, where floor-to-ceiling glass windows give you panoramic views across Blackpool and beyond.

If you're feeling fearless, why not try the Skywalk? The only thing separating you from the town below is a panel of glass. It's the closest you'll ever get to walking on air!

Sticker Scores

5 TERRIFIC TOWER

4 CRACKING COLUMN

3 SOUND STRUCTURE

2 SPINDLY SPIRE

1 PATHETIC PILLAR

Top Tip

Look out for the Blackpool Illuminations! Over a million bulbs are used to flood the promenade with light and colour from September to November.

Photo Op

Have your picture taken lying on the Skywalk – it'll look like you're floating on air!

Best Of The Rest

🗝️ Get executed at the Blackpool Tower Dungeon. The despicable dungeon is one of eight attractions inside the tower. As well as the Eye, there's also a world-famous ballroom, circus and indoor play area.

🗝️ Play mini golf at Pirate Adventure Mini Golf. This pirate-themed course takes you around cannons, rock tunnels, rigging and treasure. It's perfect for aspiring adventure golfers!

🗝️ Master the Masterblaster at Blackpool's *flum*-ongous Sandcastle Waterpark. It's the longest indoor roller-coaster waterslide in the world! www.sandcastle-waterpark.co.uk

Fascinating Facts

⭐ **Blackpool Tower is modelled on the world-famous Eiffel Tower in Paris. The town's mayor got an *eif*-full of the original on a trip to France and decided to build his own version back in Blackpool.**

Make A Day Of It

🗝️ Hand-feed birds at Martin Mere. There are almost 100 species in this wonder-*fowl* wetlands centre, and many will nibble from your hand. You can buy bags of grain from the information desk. www.wwt.org.uk

PLAN YOUR VISIT 97

The Blackpool Tower
The Promenade, Blackpool, FY1 4BJ
www.theblackpooltower.com

📞 **01253 622242**

🕐 **Daily**

£££*

*It's cheaper if you book online

I want to go here ☐

TAKE A STEAM-TRAIN RIDE

...on the Ravenglass and Eskdale Railway

You might not think that steam does much apart from come out of kettles. However, in the old days it was used to power entire trains!

The Ravenglass and Eskdale Railway runs for seven miles (about 40 minutes) through some of the Lake District's prettiest valleys. You ride in an open-air carriage on a real, working miniature steam train. There are also covered carriages if it's raining – which happens quite a lot in the Lake District! The railway has a nickname, La'al Ratty, which means 'little narrow way'. It has four small working steam engines called Irt, Mite, Esk (all named after rivers) and Northern Rock.

Sticker Scores

5 — FAT CONTROLLER

4 — STATION MASTER

3 — ENGINE DRIVER

2 — GRUMPY GUARD

1 — PENNILESS PASSENGER

Make A Day Of It

🔑 Get spooked at nearby Muncaster Castle, which claims to be one of the most haunted places in England. It's also home to the World Owl Centre, which has one of the best owl collections in the world. Sounds twit-*twoo* good to be true! www.muncaster.co.uk

🔑 Go beachcombing for gems at St Bees Head. The shingle beach is a treasure trove of semi-precious stones – look out for striped agate and bright-red jasper. www.visitcumbria.com

Top Tip
Buy an Explorer ticket for unlimited travel, and you can hop on and off at any of the line's five stations all day.

Fascinating Facts

⭐ The Arlesdale Railway in the *Thomas the Tank Engine* stories is based on the Ravenglass and Eskdale Line. The books feature the characters Bert, Rex, Mike and Jock, who are in fact named after . . . Irt, Esk, Mite and Northern Rock!

Best Of The Rest

🔑 Dalegarth is the final stop of the railway. It has a visitor centre, a shop, bike hire and a café. Dalegarth sits at the foot of England's highest mountain, Scafell Pike (978m high).

PLAN YOUR VISIT 98

Ravenglass and Eskdale Railway
Ravenglass, CA18 1SW
www.ravenglass-railway.co.uk
📞 **01229 717171**
🕐 **Check website for timetables**

£ – ££

I want to go here ☐

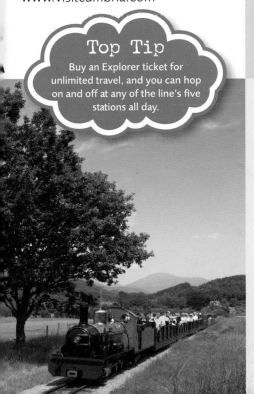

...on Lake Windermere

Lake Windermere is so big that it actually has its own tide! It is the largest natural lake in England and makes the other ones in the Lake District seem like ponds in comparison.

You can explore the lake by catching one of the boats run by Windermere Lake Cruises. At ten and a half miles long and one mile wide, the lake is ideal for a leisurely cruise. Along the way you'll see isolated islands, thick forests, bustling boatyards and fantastic fells.

Start your journey at Bowness, Lakeside or Ambleside.

Sticker Scores

| 5 LARGE LAKE | 4 TERRIFIC TARN | 3 MIDDLING MOAT |
| 2 PIDDLING POND | 1 PATHETIC PUDDLE | |

You'll be able to choose anything from a quick 45 minute island cruise to a Freedom of the Lake pass for serious Windermere explorers.

Which vegetable would you never want in your boat?

A leek!

Make A Day Of It

🔑 Follow your nose to Sarah Nelson's famous gingerbread shop in Grasmere. It's next to St Oswald's Church, which is the burial place of the famous poet William Wordsworth. www.grasmeregingerbread.co.uk

Similar Spots

🔑 Hire a rowing boat in Fell Foot Park, at the southern end of Lake Windermere. The huge lawns next to the lake are great for picnics and there's a top adventure playground too. www.nationaltrust.org.uk

🔑 Go on a gondola on Coniston Water. This rebuilt Victorian steam yacht is a bit like the gondolas of Venice, but bigger and powered by steam instead of arm muscle! www.nationaltrust.org.uk

Fascinating Facts

⭐ **Over 1,000 years ago, a vain Viking called Vinand decided to name the large lake he discovered after . . . himself! Over time Vinand's Mere (an old word for lake) became better known as Windermere.**

⭐ The Vikings first arrived in Cumbria in around 925 A.D. and occupied the area for almost 300 years. You can still see (and hear) their influence in some of the words used to describe the geographical features of the Lake District. Fell (see p220), ghyll (meaning waterfall) and beck (meaning stream) all originate from the Viking language of Old Norse.

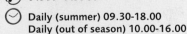

PLAN YOUR VISIT (99)

Windermere Lake Cruises
Bowness Pier, Bowness-on-Windermere, LA23 3HQ
www.windermere-lakecruises.co.uk

📞 **01539 443360**

🕐 **Daily (summer) 09.30-18.00**
Daily (out of season) 10.00-16.00

££

I want to go here ☐

CLIMB UP A FELL

...at Orrest Head

A fell is a local word for a large hill. When in the Lake District it would be rude not to climb at least one. So why not start with one of the most famous fell walks and climb Orrest Head?

Orrest Head has one of the best views in the Lake District. On a clear day, from the top you can see Windermere, Morecambe Bay, central Lakeland and even the Yorkshire Dales. That's a lot of view from one spot!

It takes about twenty minutes to walk to the top from Windermere Station.

On your way you'll pass through the beautiful Elleray Wood, where you'll find a blacksmith's workshop. There are also benches along the route if you need a breather.

Sticker Scores

5 AWESOME ADVENTURER

4 FEARLESS FELLWALKER

3 HEROIC HIKER

2 TOILING TREKKER

1 FELL OVER

Why doesn't a fell get cold in the winter? It has a snow *cap*!

Make A Day Of It

🔑 Hire a bike and explore beautiful Grizedale Forest. There are five cycle trails, as well as woodland walking routes.

🔑 Cuddle up to Peter Rabbit at the World of Beatrix Potter. Peter and his furry and feathered friends come to life in this indoor re-creation of the Lakeland countryside.
www.hop-skip-jump.com

Similar Spots

🔑 Trek to the top of the Old Man of Coniston – an 800 metre high mountain with spectacular views from the summit. Follow the well-marked route from Coniston village, and allow four hours for the round trip.

Fascinating Facts

★ **The Wainwrights are the 214 fells described in Alfred Wainwright's famous fell-walking guides. The youngest person to scale all the Wainwright peaks was just five years old at the time!**

★ The highest mountain in England is Scafell Pike, in the Lake District. It's 978 metres tall, which makes it higher than 650 giant pike fish stacked head to tail (but much less smelly!).

Top Tip

Keep your strength up with some Kendal mint cake from nearby Kendal. This local speciality is basically a bar of sugar which is sometimes coated in chocolate. This makes it fine fodder for fuelling fell-walkers!

PLAN YOUR VISIT (100)

Orrest Head
Windermere, LA23
www.english-lakes.com

FREE

I want to go here ☐

WATCH A 3D FILM INSIDE A HILL

...at the Rheged Centre

The Rheged Centre is Europe's largest grass-covered building. OK, so there might not be too much competition for that title. But we still think it will leave the other contenders *green* with envy!

Rheged is an awesome activity centre just east of the Lake District. It has been built to look like a Lakeland hill, complete with crags, waterfalls and a whole lot of grass. Best of all, it's equipped with a massive 3D movie screen!

The 3D cinema is as tall as six double-decker buses, so you feel like you're in the centre of all the action.

Sticker Scores

5	4	3
HEAVENLY HILL	MASSIVE MOUND	FANCY FELL

2	1
PIFFLING PROMONTORY	OVER THE HILL

Sit back and watch dinosaurs fight around you, or let fish swim through your fingertips. Just don't try growing a garden on your roof when you get home!

Make A Day Of It

🔑 Stand above a waterfall at Aira Force. It's one of the most spectacular sights in the Lakes. www.national-trust.org.uk

🔑 Ride a horse near Ullswater, England's second largest lake. Park Foot Trekking centre offers escorted treks around beautiful countryside overlooking the lake. www.parkfootponytrekking.co.uk

What do dogs eat at the cinema?
Pup-corn!

Fascinating Facts

★ Rheged was originally the name of the ancient kingdom of Cumbria which existed during the sixth century. At that time it was one of the most powerful parts of the land and covered most of North West England.

★ Covering buildings in grass is more common than you might think. For thousands of years people have used straw (a form of dried long grass) to make thatched roofs.

PLAN YOUR VISIT 101

Rheged Centre
Redhills, Penrith, CA11 0DQ
www.rheged.com

📞 01768 868000

🕐 Daily 10.00-17.30
Films hourly 11.00-16.00

££ (films)   £ (other activities)

I want to go here ☐

NORTH WEST

...at the Bowder Stone

Unless you want to be squished we strongly suggest you don't actually try to balance a 2,000 tonne stone on your fingertip! But, by using camera trickery, you can create a pretty convincing photo.

The extraordinary Bowder Stone in the Borrowdale Valley is the largest standing stone in the Lake District. At ten metres high and sixteen metres wide it is bigger than a terraced house! Incredibly, it somehow balances on one corner, giving the impression that it could topple over any second.

Stand beneath the stone and reach up to touch it. You will create the illusion that you are balancing the boulder on your fingertip! There's also a ladder resting against the stone so that you can climb up and sit on top of it.

Sticker Scores

5 BRILLIANT BOULDER

4 SUPER STONE

3 MYSTERIOUS MOUND

2 REASONABLE ROCK

1 PATHETIC PEBBLE

Make A Day Of It

 Go rock climbing at Honister Slate Mine. If you're ten years old (and at least 1.3 metres tall) you can climb the Via Ferrata, England's first ever adventure climbing system. The highest point is a spine-tingling 600 metres up in the air!
www.honister-slate-mine.co.uk

 Stroke a snake at the Reptile Encounter in Trotters World of Animals. This place has oodles of unusual animals, from Asian fishing cats to mandrills (the world's largest monkey species).
www.trottersworld.com

What came after the Stone Age and the Bronze Age?
The saus-age!

Fascinating Facts

★ The Bowder Stone is known by geologists as a perched rock. It was transported to Borrowdale from a long way away (probably from Scotland) on a glacier. When the glaciers melted at the end of the Ice Age it 'perched' in its current lopsided position. So, as it's been that way for thousands of years you can be reassured that it's pretty safe!

★ Victorians, who loved visiting the stone, believed it had tumbled down from the crags above. Mind you, the Victorians also believed that draining blood from someone's body was a good way to cure disease, so they're probably not the most reliable source of information!

PLAN YOUR VISIT 102

Bowder Stone
Near Grange-in-Borrowdale, Keswick, Cumbria
www.visitcumbria.com

FREE NT

I want to go here ☐

TOP FIVE

...animal encounters

If you're keen on cuddly creatures, or fanatical about feathered friends, you'll love these amazing animal encounters.

I WENT TO:

- [ ] **Cheshire Falconry**
- [ ] **Banham Zoo**
- [ ] **South Lakes Wild Animal Park**
- [ ] **Dartmoor Zoo**
- [ ] **Livingstone Lodge**

Cheshire Falconry

Cheshire Falconry is home to over 60 birds of prey, from elegant eagles to fine falcons.

Owl enthusiasts will enjoy the Junior Owl Experience, which lets you get up close to these wise winged wonders. The best bit is when a beautiful barn owl lands on your hand! (Don't worry, you'll be wearing gloves to protect you from their tough talons.) You'll have a wonderf-*owl* day!

Cheshire Falconry

Blakemere Craft Centre, Chester Road, Northwich, CW8 2EB
www.cheshirefalconry.com
01606 882223

Banham Zoo

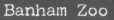

Banham Zoo has almost a thous: animals, but we're to *stick our neck o* and say that the gir are our favourites!

For an extra fee on top your ticket, you can ha feed the giraffes. Give their size, this would normally be a *tall* order but the zoo has a speci platform you can stand to dish out the delights It's the most ex-*height* part of the day!

Banham Zoo

Kenninghall Road, Banham,
www.banhamzoo.co
01953 887771

outh Lakes ld Animal rk

Dartmoor Zoo

Livingstone Lodge

outh Lakes Wild Animal Park is the y place in Europe ere you can see ers hunting for food. a spectacular sight!

e big cats climb a six-tre pole to grab meat that been placed at the top. s keeps them fit and also mics how they'd hunt for d in the wild. So it's like ch and a PE lesson all ed into one!

uth Lakes Wild imal Park

ughton Road, Dalton in Furness, 5 8JR

w.wildanimalpark.co.uk

229 466086

In 2006, Benjamin Mee went looking for a nice family home in the countryside . . . and ended up buying a zoo!

The story of how the Mee family purchased Dartmoor Zoological Park has now been turned into a Hollywood film called *We Bought A Zoo*. But before you watch the film, why not visit the real thing? The zoo is set in a beautiful part of Dartmoor and has an impressive selection of big cats.

Dartmoor Zoological Park

Sparkwell, Plymouth PL7 5DG

www.dartmoorzoo.org

01752 837645

Livingstone Lodge in Kent is the UK's first overnight safari experience. It's *zoo*-nique!

If you're nine or older, you and your family can spend a night under the stars in one of the lodge's terrific tents. You'll wake up to see wild animals like zebra and wildebeest grazing and drinking at the nearby watering hole. It's like being on safari in Africa, so you'll have to pinch yourself to remember you're in a tent in Kent!

Livingstone Safari Lodge

Port Lympne Wild Animal & Safari Park, Lympne, Nr Hythe, CT21 4PD

www.aspinallfoundation.org

0844 842 4647

TOP FIVE

...sporting days out

If you follow football or rave about rugby, you'll know England's sporting teams don't always finish in first place. But we still think these sporting days out are real *winners*!

I WENT TO:

- [ ] Twickenham Stadium
- [ ] Twenty20
- [ ] Santa Pod Raceway
- [ ] Football Stadium Tour
- [ ] Wimbledon Lawn Tennis Museum

Twickenham Stadium

Twickenham Stadium has been the home of English rugby since 1910, when it held a crowd of 20,000 people. Today it can seat four times as many!

Take the Twickenham Stadium tour and you'll get to step into the players' dressing rooms (hopefully they'll have picked up their sweaty socks!) and walk onto the pitch. Then head over to the museum to test your strength on the scrum machine. Crouch, touch, pause . . . ENGAGE!

Twickenham Stadium
Rugby Road, Twickenham, TW1 1DZ
www.rfu.com
020 8892 8877

Twenty20

Twenty20 is a shorter, more action-packed form cricket (the bat and game, not the insec

Teams play in the t20 le which runs in the summ - check www.ecb.co.uk upcoming fixtures. Ther often music and other entertainment, so you w be *stumped* for things t keep you amused. And matches never last more a few hours (unlike regu cricket games), you're a unlikely to end up with numb bum!

www.ecb.co.uk

nta Pod ceway

Football Stadium Tour

Wimbledon Lawn Tennis Museum

anta Pod Raceway is the home of UK drag ing – the fastest (and siest) motorsport in e world!

can watch cars and torcycles tearing around illy speeds on regular e days. Or why not catch e of the action-packed ws? Stunt Fest has vities, fireworks and edevil deeds, while Flame hunder features monster cks and jet vehicles. With his excitement, we're e your day won't *drag* on!

nta Pod Raceway
eld Road, Podington,
lingborough, NN29 7XA
w.santapod.com
234 782828

Whichever team you support, we reckon nothing tops this turf tour!

Wembley is the home of English football and one of the most famous stadiums in the world, so it's a terrific place to take a tour. Many Premiership clubs also offer their own behind-the-scenes experience, including access to players' and managers' areas and a stroll onto the pitch. Whichever one you choose, you're sure to have a *ball*!

Wembley National Stadium
Wembley, HA9 0WS
www.wembleystadium.com
0844 800 2755

If you're a tennis fan, you'll *love* the Wimbledon tour.

The world-famous Wimbledon Championships are held every summer and you need tickets for the tennis to visit during that period. But for the rest of the year you can go on the official tour, which takes in Centre Court (where the biggest matches are played), the interview room and the on-site museum. Get set for a great day out!

Wimbledon Lawn Tennis Museum
All England Lawn Tennis & Croquet Club, Church Road, Wimbledon, SW19 5AE
www.wimbledon.org
020 8946 6131

TOP FIVE

...fun journeys

Not all journeys are as boring as the school run. Here are our top tips for top trips!

Burgh Island Sea Tractor

Dudley Canal Trust Trips

Boats travel through water and tractors trundle over ground. Except for the Burgh Island sea tractor, that is, because *it* does both!

The sea tractor ferries people to tiny Burgh Island – a chunk of land off the Devon coast that gets cut off from the mainland at high tide. You'll power along on a giant platform with the waves lapping at your feet, before hopping off for a roam around the island. This is one tractor with added wow factor!

Burgh Island Hotel
Burgh Island, Kingsbridge, TQ7 4BG
www.burghisland.com
01548 810514

Board a barge on Dudley Canal and you'll discover spooky undergroun network of man-ma tunnels and cavern

You'll watch an *illuminati* sound and light show in Singing Cavern and see a legging demonstration. (has nothing to do with ti trousers – legging is the miners used to move thro the canals before boats became motorised.) We' sure you'll agree that the nothing banal about this

Dudley Canal Trus
Birmingham New Road, DY
www.dudleycanaltrust
01384 236275

oseph's nazing amels

Pesky Husky

Virgin Balloon Flights

With Joseph's Amazing Camels u can trek through the tswold countryside on mel-back!

e three-hour experience rts with tea and biscuits. ce you've fuelled up, u'll groom your camel and ap on the saddle before velling to the starting nt of the trek. Riding a nel can actually be quite axing. But don't take our rd for it – camel-long and e for yourself!

seph's Amazing amels

e Old Farm House, Whitehouse m, Idliecote, CV36 5DN
ww.jacamels.co.uk
608 66136

Picture yourself speeding along with the wind in your hair pulled by a pack of huskies. Are you in the Artic? No, you're in Scarborough!

At Pesky Husky Trekking you get to ride on a cool scooter while being pulled along by these adorable dogs. As the huskies love the cold, trekking only takes place during winter months, but you can go hiking with the dogs or take a kennel tour all year round.

Pesky Husky

Meeting House Farm, Staintondale, Scarborough, YO23 0EL
www.peskyhusky.co.uk
01723 870521

Take a trip with Virgin Balloon Flights and you could find yourself flying above England's amazing countryside!

Virgin Balloon Flights have sites all over the UK. Make sure you take your camera – you'd be a loon not to take photos in a balloon! Our favourite location is Lancashire's stunning Forest of Bowland. You'll help with the inflation of the big balloon before boarding the basket and floating off. It's an un-fir-gettable experience!

Virgin Balloon Flights

Stonyhurst College, Clitheroe, BB7 9PZ
Other locations across country
www.virginballoonflights.co.uk
01952 212750

TOP FIVE

...places to feast on food

England has some delicious delicacies, so it's tricky to choose five favourites. Nonetheless, here are some taste-bud-tickling treats!

Stein's Fish & Chips

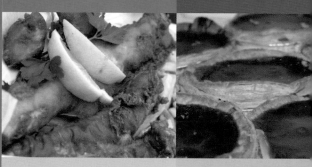

We can't think of a better *plaice* to feast on a fish supper than beside the boats in Padstow Harbour.

Padstow is a pretty Cornish fishing town that's home to several superb seafood spots. We suggest picking up a takeaway from Stein's Fish & Chips on South Quay and heading for the harbour. Watch out for herring boats and lobster catchers – and be careful the seagulls don't steal your supper!

Stein's Fish & Chips
South Quay, Padstow, PL28 8BL
www.rickstein.com
01841 532700

Bakewell Pudding Sho

The Derbyshire town of Bakewe home to the Bakew Pudding – a deliciou jam pastry with a ri almondy filling.

Confusingly, Bakewell T don't actually come fror Bakewell. So if you want traditional treat, the pud is hard to beat. Try one i the Bakewell Pudding Sh – they're served hot with cream or custard. Now t what we call baking well

The Old Original Bakewell Pudding
The Square, Bakewell, Derb
www.bakewellpuddin.co.uk
01629 812193

artmel illage Shop

Wensleydale Creamery

Lizard Pasty Shop

▶ticky Toffee Pudding is a super sponge cake vered in toffee sauce ich comes from the ke District. It's perfect refuelling after a long y of trekking.

ere's no doubt that the sion sold at Cartmel in the uth of the Lake District is ply sensational. Its perfect ds are world-famous and to international customers all shapes and sizes (the ddings, not the customers!).

artmel Village Shop
xgate House, The Square, tmel, LA11 6QB
vw.cartmelvillageshop. uk
539 536280

I f you're keen on crumbly, creamy cheese, you can't fail with a piece of Wensleydale!

Wensleydale Cheese has been made in the Yorkshire Dales for over 1,000 years. It's also the favourite cheese of Wallace from the Wallace and Gromit films. You can learn all about the cheese-making process at the Wensleydale Creamery, before heading off to sample the finished article in the tasting room. *Dale*-icious!

Wensleydale Creamery
Gayle Lane, Hawes, DL8 3RN
www.wensleydale.co.uk
01969 667664

N o trip to Cornwall is complete without polishing off a pasty.

The Cornish Pasty (or 'oggy', as it's called in Cornish) is a semi-circular meat pie with a thick crust. It started life as a lunch for tin miners, who would hold the crust with their grubby hands while scoffing the tasty filling. You can buy oggies all over Cornwall, but we think the Lizard Pasty Shop in Lizard village serves particularly perfect parcels of pastry.

Lizard Pasty Shop
Sunny Corner, Beacon Terrace, The Lizard, TR12 7PB
www.annspasties.co.uk
01326 290889

TOP FIVE

...cool collections

If you've ever collected anything, we reckon you'll have respect for these humongous hoards and cool collections.

I WENT TO:

- [ ] Horniman Museum and Gardens
- [ ] Norwich Castle
- [ ] Hat Works
- [ ] The Museum of Childhood
- [ ] The Cumberland Pencil Museum

Horniman Museum and Gardens

The Horniman is a fascinating museum that's filled with anything and everything!

The museum says that it promotes understanding of the world. We say it's got loads of cool stuff and you have to see it to appreciate it! We love the Music Gallery, which has 12,000 weird and wonderful instruments on display. Try out the dulcimer – a sort of cross between a xylophone and a banjo. It's *strum*-thing special!

Horniman Museum
100 London Road, SE23 3PQ
www.horniman.ac.uk
020 8699 1872

Norwich Cas

Norwich Castle i fine fortress th was built to defend city against invasion It also has the world largest collection of ceramic teapots!

There are over 3,000 tea in the Twining Teapot Gallery. They come in all sorts of shapes – there's war tank, a cabbage, a c and even a monkey. The sizes also vary from tea-n tiny to pret-*tea* large. Yo be *potty* to miss it!

Norwich Castle
Castle Meadow, Norwich, NR
www.museums.norfolk
01603 493625

at Works

The Museum of Childhood

The Cumberland Pencil Museum

Hat Works in Stockport has a ~~tty~~ hat collection ~~hat~~ has to be seen to ~~believed!~~

~~t~~ Works is set in a cool ~~ctorian~~ mill building which ~~s~~ once a thriving hat ~~tory.~~ There are all kinds ~~hats~~ on display, from ~~lliant~~ bowlers to trendy ~~bies.~~ Best of all, there's ~~en~~ a dressing-up room ~~ere~~ you can try some on ~~size.~~ *Head* over there ~~d~~ see for yourself!

The Museum of Childhood is all about kids, so unlike some museums, it's full of interesting things that are actually interesting, like toys and games.

The museum is a treasure trove of toys from all ages. You can watch toy trains and make a robot come to life in the Toy Gallery, or marvel at the huge collection of doll's houses. The museum also offers daily art activities, so you might just find inspiration for some crafty creations of your own!

We reckon The Cumberland Pencil Museum in Keswick is one of the *sharpest* attractions around!

The museum's main attraction is the world's largest coloured pencil. At almost eight metres long, it's twice the length of a boa constrictor (though less likely to squeeze a pig to death!). Head to the Drawing Zone, where you can get creative and even draw on the walls. We don't recommend trying that at home, though!

at Works

~~llington~~ Mill, Wellington Road ~~th,~~ Stockport, SK3 0EU

~~w.~~hatworks.org.uk

~~61~~ 355 7770

V&A Museum of Childhood

Cambridge Heath Road, E2 9PA

www.vam.ac.uk/moc

020 8983 5200

The Cumberland Pencil Museum

Southey Works, Keswick, CA12 5NG

www.pencilmuseum.co.uk

01768 773626

PARENTS' PAGE

Greetings, adult. This page is all for you. The rest of the book's for kids, so we thought it was only fair that you had your own page. So if you're a child, stop reading. Now. We said stop. Look, the whole rest of the book's for you. This is just for adults. There's tons more interesting things to do in the rest of the book – for example, why not go to p56 and find out where you can watch racing pigs? In fact, we suggest you do anything but read this page. Stop reading right this second. Are you still there? No. Good.

So anyway, hello, adult.

England Unlocked is for children who are visiting places with adults. Very few of our sites admit unaccompanied children. So as you're likely to be the one planning the trip, we've included site details, such as telephone numbers and opening hours, on each page. Bear in mind that most sites are closed for Christmas, and that last admission is usually earlier than the closing time. We've also specified if there are height or age restrictions. While we have tried hard to ensure all the details are accurate at the time of going to press, things change, so it's best to check before you go anywhere.

Next: the Internet. We've tried to make sure that all our websites are child-friendly, but all the same, we suggest you supervise any surfing. We take no responsibility for third-party content and we recommend you check a site first if you are at all unsure.

Now for some general tips:

- Quite a few venues run good workshops and activities during weekends and school holidays. These are sometimes free, but may require advance booking.
- Many of the activities can be combined into a single day out. Use the maps at the beginning of each section to work out what things are near each other.
- Some of the activities in our book could be dangerous without appropriate adult supervision. Children using this book should be accompanied at all times.
- Many of our free activities in England involve walks or other locations which don't have opening hours. We recommend you only go during daylight, and make sure you leave enough time to complete the walks.

Oh, and we think it's worth us mentioning that none of the sites in this book pay to be included.

Right then, that's the practical stuff out the way, and there's still a page to fill. So we've selected some facts about England just for grown ups. We don't think they're as interesting as the facts in the rest of the book, but then being an adult you don't really like interesting facts do you now?

- England has a temperate maritime climate, with temperatures usually staying between 0 °C and 30 °C. However, the mild conditions do not stop the English from obsessing about whether it is too warm, too cold or too rainy.
- England is part of the United Kingdom of Great Britain and Northern Ireland, which is possibly the most boringly long-winded name of any country in the world. It's no wonder most people just shorten this to 'UK'.
- The UK has an uncodified constitution (as opposed to a written one). This means that there is no single document containing it. Instead it is embodied in statutes, court judgments, treaties and many other types of boring document that we can't be bothered to list.
- The UK is a constitutional monarchy, meaning that the head of state is a king or queen. Currently the monarch is Queen Elizabeth, and her heir apparent is Prince Charles. He should not be confused with her apparent hair, which is on her head.
- England has a population of a little over 51 million people. Seven million of these live in London, meaning 14% of the population live in England's capital city.
- At a little over 50,000 square miles, England is almost exactly the same size as the American state of Alabama. Both places also contain a city called Birmingham. However, only one of them is the subject of a song describing the place as a 'sweet home'.
- England's motto is 'Dieu et mon Droit', which means 'God and my Right'. We think this is much more boring that our motto, which is 'Don't be boring, go exploring!'.
- No part of England is more than 70 miles from the coast. The furthest point from the sea is the village of Coton in the Elms, in Derbyshire. It looks like a nice place, but we haven't included it in this book as we can't find any fun things for kids to do there.
- ENGLAND UNLOCKED is an anagram of LUCK GLADDEN NONE.

OK, that's your lot. Time to hand the book back to your child. Or, if you are a child who's read all of this, we hope you learned that reading stuff meant for adults just isn't going to be very funny.

BACK-OF-THE-BOOK QUIZ

Good Luck!

The answers to all the following questions can be found somewhere in *England Unlocked*. Email a correct set of answers to us and you'll have a chance to win a signed and framed illustration of your choice from the book!

1 Where is the UK's tallest roller-coaster?

2 How many former Archbishops of Canterbury have been murdered?

3 What form of transport would you use to get to Burgh Island?

4 Who was the first man to swim the English Channel and how did he die?

5 Why does Queen Victoria always look miserable in photos?

6 According to legend, how many cups of hot chocolate did Emperor Montezuma drink in a day?

A. 5
B. 15
C. 50

7 Who wrote the first knock knock joke?

A. William Shakespeare
B. Charles Dickens
C. Emily Kerr & Joshua Perry

8 Where were the oldest rocks on Earth (from four billion years ago) found?

A. Canterbury
B. Canada
C. Canberra

9 What was the destination of the world's longest ever pizza delivery journey?

A. The Isle of Man
B. Birmingham
C. The Moon

10 What does 'Dieu et mon Droit' (England's motto) mean?

A. God save the Queen
B. God and my right
C. We reserve the right to moan about the weather

Tie-breaker

In no more than 30 words tell us what is your favourite place in the book and why.

Send your answers to **quiz@factfinderguides.co.uk**
Full terms and conditions are on our website.

ABOUT US

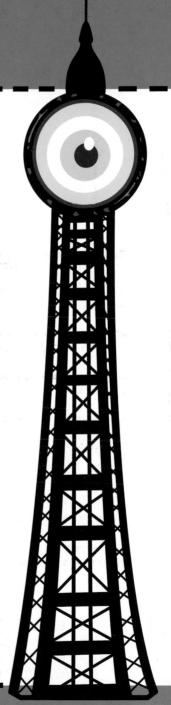

Tessa Girvan

Tessa Girvan is an author and mum from Cheshire. She is a big fan of coffee, cake and a good walk, so her favourite places in England tend to involve all three. She has learnt a lot from writing this book, and not least that the best way to see Liverpool is on board a duck with wheels.

Allison Curtis

Allison loves dogs and used to own two ducks, called Francis & Firkin. She was once part of a successful world record to have the most people bouncing on space hoppers at the same time.

Katherine Hardy (Kardy)

Kardy always wanted to have a pet pony. That would have been easier if she didn't live in central London. Quentin Blake has described her drawings as 'strong and subtly nuanced'. This is also not a bad description of her personality.

Vicky Scott

Victoria Scott decided she was going to be an illustrator when she was five years old. Apart from drawing she likes collecting coloured paper and meeting cats. People say she looks a bit like a cartoon character. She quite likes this.

Joshua Perry and Emily Kerr

Josh and Emily were at school together, which they think is a great start for setting up a children's publishing company.

They enjoy Unlocked more than any other jobs they've had. That's because their other jobs haven't involved hanging out with kids, writing dodgy puns, and visiting cool places.

LONDON

SOUTH EAST

SOUTH WEST

EAST

MIDLANDS

NORTH EAST

NORTH WEST

TOP FIVES

CREDITS

Author: Tessa Girvan **Contributors:** Mary Scott, Chloe Jeffries, Owen Williams, Katie Potter, Alexandra Tilley Loughrey, Deborah Done **Series Editors:** Joshua Perry, Emily Kerr **Design:** Allison Curtis **Illustrations:** Katherine Hardy, Vicky Scott
Maps: Allison Curtis, with reference to OpenStreetMap – a free, editable map of the world

Thank you to ...

Tessa

Richard and Molly and Mum and Dad for your endless support and enthusiasm. Five gold stars to these brilliant people for their invaluable help and advice: Nadine & Tony Darke-Partridge, Paul & Karen, Peter Girvan, Linda & Sam Graham, Emma Gray, Jane & John Holmes, Maroushka Lawrence & Eden, Rachael & Shane Kirrane, Tom Lawrie-Fussey, Katherine West & Joe, Barbara White and Simon & Siobhán White. Last but not least, thank you to all those at the featured sites for your help along the way.

Everyone else

Harlyn Bay, for great holidays. Company pub quizzes for keeping us entertained. Franco Manca for the best pizzas in London. Other people's cats for brightening up meetings. Our Kids Board of Directors for always being right.

Photo Credits

11 Trustees of the British Museum	99 David Broadbent	189 York Archaeological Trust
13 Stephen May	101 Joe Ashworth	191 Seven Stories
15 flickr, Maurice db	103 The Big Sheep	193 flickr, Martyn Wright
17 flickr, Heather M	105 flickr, me'nthedogs	195 Margaret Whittaker
19 flickr, César Astudillo	107 flickr, kullez	197 Flickr, Steenbergs
21 flickr, César Astudillo	109 flickr, Visentico/sento	201 Chester Zoo
23 Merlin Entertainments	111 flickr, jooliargh	203 Hack Green
25 Peter Smith / St. Paul's Cathedral	113 flickr, Kai Hendry	205 Blue Planet
27 Frantzesco Kangaris	115 flickr, cloudsoup	207 Roger Sinek, Tate Liverpool 2011
29 Admas Habteslasie	117 Eden Project	209 Yellow Duckmarine
31 Natural History Museum	119 flickr, a.froese	211 Chris Foster/MOSI
33 flickr, billfromesm	121 NTPL/David Norton	213 jlcwalkcr
35 flickr, Matt Brown	123 Splashdown Water Park	215 Blackpool Tower
37 flickr, mallsecrets	127 Rebecca Walton	217 Ravenglass and Eskdale Railway
39 flickr, Les Chatfield	129 flickr, sarah	219 Windermere Lake Cruises
41 Wimbledon Lawn Tennis Museum	131 flickr, ndrwfgg	221 flickr, David Picker
43 Jonathan Brady	133 St Edmundsbury Borough Council Heritage	223 Rheged
45 flickr, Stephen Boisvert	Service	225 flickr, Darren Teagles
47 flickr, Mark Kobayashi-Hillary	135 flickr, Martin Pettit	226 flickr, Peter G Trimming
49 flickr, David Blaikie	137 flickr, Arfrazh	226 flickr, StuBez
51 flickr, Andy Dudley	139 flickr, Ell Brown	227 South Lakes Wildlife Park
55 Merlin Entertainments	141 Bean's Seal Trips	227 flickr, S Baker
57 Bocketts Farm	145 Richard Aldred	227 flickr, alex_lee2001
59 flickr, sonewfangled	147 Liz West	228 World Rugby Museum
61 Canterbury Cathedral	149 Wendy Jackson	228 Flickr, Nick Townsend
63 Kyle Taylor, Dream it. Do it. World Tour	151 flickr, Ell Brown	229 Flickr, tharrin
65 Merlin Entertainments	153 Cadbury World	229 flickr, Andy Dudley
67 New Forest National Park Authority	155 Jim Linwood	229 Wimbledon Lawn Tennis Museum
69 Portsmouth Historic Dockyard	157 Falstaff's Experience	230 flickr, Didby Graham
71 Pelican Racing	159 flickr, Steve p2008	230 Dudley Canal Trust
73 Pitt Rivers	161 Heights of Abraham	231 Joseph's Camels
75 2011 Warner Bros. Ent. Harry Potter Publishing	163 flickr, eamoncurry123	231 flickr, HerPhotographer
Rights J.K.R	165 flickr, Duncan	231 flickr, Kilgarron
77 Oxford Castle Unlocked	167 National Space Centre, Leicester	232 Rick Stein's Seafood Restaurant
81 Tony Kerr	169 Gibraltar Point	232 Bakewell pudding
83 At-Bristol	173 National Media Museum Bradford	233 Cartmel Village Shop
85 Bath & North East Somerset Council	175 Diggerland	233 flickr, EJB-Photography
87 Andrew Desmond	177 flickr, Martyn Wright	233 Cornish pasty
89 flickr, Elliott Brown	179 Mary Wills	234 Laura Mtungwazi / Horniman Museum
91 flickr, Lawrie Cate	181 Log Heights	234 Norwich Castle
93 Longleat	183 Dee Maddams, Neptuno Photography	235 Hatworks
95 WWT Slimbridge Wetland Centre	185 National Railway Museum	235 V&A Museum of Childhood
97 Cotswold Farm Park	187 Vindolanda	235 Alex Spencer